SCOTLAND: FREQUENTLY ASKED QUESTIONS

What every visitor needs to know

DERRICK WHITE

www.theinpinn.co.uk

ACKNOWLEDGEMENTS
My thanks to Bernice for her
hawk-eyed proof reading.

Thanks also to Gray Line and Timberbush Tours for
giving me the opportunity to meet so many
interesting people.

BOOKS BY THE SAME AUTHOR
Close More Sales
Success With Psycometric Testing
Knowing You, Knowing Me
Close More Sales (Revised)

The In Pinn
is an imprint of
Neil Wilson Publishing Ltd
303 The Pentagon Centre
36 Washington Street
GLASGOW
G3 8AZ

Tel: 0141-221-1117
Fax: 0141-221-5363
E-mail: info@nwp.co.uk
www.nwp.co.uk

A catalogue record for this book is available
from the British Library.

ISBN 1-903238-59-5

Typeset in LucidaSans
Printed by CPD

CONTENTS

Chapter 4. Religion

Chapter 5. Food, Drink and Tourist Thoughts

Chapter 1
Pursuits and Recreations

Q: What is trainspotting?

A: It is a measure of our insularity that we presume that the rest of the world understands what trainspotting is, however, it is a singularly British (more precisely English) piece of eccentricity. Trainspotters can be found on the platforms of the great centres of railway activity such as Clapham Junction in London or Crewe in the English Midlands. Their hobby is to record the serial numbers of trains – the more rare or exotic the better. *What for?* This is one of the great unsolved mysteries of the universe, like fluffy dice. *Are you saying fluffy dice?* Later, later! Of the spotter we can only guess; perhaps as bird watchers can tell one another that they have seen a Lesser Spotted Throat Warbler, the trainspotters can boast that they have seen a ZX92K. Who knows?

Q: I was confused by the movie's title?

A: Not surprisingly. The author of the book, Irvine Welsh, chose the title Trainspotting, as an exercise in irony. The term Trainspotting conjures up images of the most innocent and unworldly types pursuing their wholly innocuous hobby. The title juxtaposed with a group of drug taking, thieving drop-outs from an Edinburgh housing scheme is part of the sardonic humour which runs through the book and the movie. *Sardonic?* Yes, Welsh himself was brought up in Muirhouse, one of Edinburgh's peripheral housing schemes and throughout his book there are the two conflicting messages — the bourgeois theme of acquisitive aspiration and the reality of a hopeless underclass.

Q: Are there no trainspotters in Scotland?

A: Not in any significant numbers. Sightings have been made at Glasgow Central, Edinburgh Waverley and on occasion at Falkirk but it was the very passive Englishness of the pursuit which Welsh used to heighten his message of irony.

Q: ISN'T THERE ALSO AN AERONAUTICAL EQUIVALENT – THE PLANESPOTTER?

A: Yes, rumour has it they gather at Terminal Two at Heathrow Airport to record and photograph the world's aircraft.

But surely one Boeing 747 looks very much like another? You asked what the pursuit was; why people do it is perhaps a matter for the psychoanalyst.

Why, are these people nuts? Oh no, that would be too unkind but they are certainly different. So much so that they have been given nicknames such as anoraks or nerds. *Anoraks?* It is said to come from the essential trainspotting garb. Squatting at the end of a cold and windy platform writing down numbers, calls for extra insulation!

But why do they do it? A consultant psychologist was interviewed on UK TV's Channel 4 News regarding twelve plane-spotters who were arrested and imprisoned in Greece. *Greek plane-spotters?* No, wait a second, these spotters were English who had travelled to Greece to an air show and were observed by the local police taking photographs of planes and recording their details. *Is that illegal?* They were arrested because Greece has a very nervy relationship with her neighbour Turkey and the spotters were recording details of military aircraft. Now, because plane-spotting is a peculiarly English form of eccentricity, the Greeks could not believe that people would travel all that way simply to record some details that they could probably find in *Jane's Military Aircraft. Why not?* Mediterranean people have three main priorities, food, drink and making love – a Greek standing at the mouth of an Aegean harbour recording numbers of fishing boats would merit sympathetic smiles and a pat on the head.

Q: SO WHY DIDN'T THESE PLANESPOTTERS JUST SIT AT HEATHROW'S TERMINAL TWO?

A: Because air shows involve military aircraft which are considered more interesting. *Okay, so what exactly did this psychologist say?* He suggested that there was a deep rooted sexual undertone in the hobby – the phallic shape of aeroplanes and their surging and thrusting power penetrating the air. *You're kidding?* Would anyone make this up! This is not to say that the psychologist was correct – he seems far too much of a Freudian to have a balanced view. The TV programme went on to interview some spotters at Terminal Two and frankly any connection with surging, thrusting, penetrating power seemed rather tenuous. A more passive and harmless type of man would be hard to find anywhere, even in passionless southern England.

Wasn't there a woman involved in this Greek thing, charged with aiding and abetting? She was there probably to hold the anoraks while the boys took the photographs. Counting things is a peculiarly male and English pastime. On, say, a Sunday in the Celtic fringe – Scotland, Ireland and Wales – people might hill-walk, build something, read or get morosely drunk on an all-day binge but the English are more likely to be counting things.

Like what? Beer mats, bottle labels, stamps, horse brasses, coins, old copies of comics or magazines, cigarette cards, war memorabilia — almost anything. On holiday they know the rate of exchange of the local currency, the temperature there (and at home), how much an English breakfast costs, the miles they walked, the height they climbed, the cost of a taxi ride, flight durations, altitude and the savings with duty-free goods. They are really good at measuring things. The Celts are more philosophic and from earliest bardic times have a deep respect for learning. The Anglo-Saxon likes to count.

Q: ARE ENGLISH SOUTHERNERS REALLY PASSIONLESS?

A: The English comedy actor John Cleese delivers a cutting attack on English inhibition in the movie A Fish Called Wanda. Cleese admitted to having difficulty in forming relationships with English women as he found the exchanges so fraught with snobbish class shibboleths and deeply ingrained inhibitions.

With American women he felt free and at ease. English southerners are nice enough people but the average southern dinner party makes people of a Celtic temperament panic. The measured tones of neutral conversation, the clink of cutlery, the restrained sipping of the wine, the silences. Europeans, Americans, the Celts all jabber away and embellish their stories with exaggerations, distortions and outright invention. Nobody cares, to them the essence of conversation is enjoyment or, to use the Gaelic word *craic*. The English are more likely to interrupt a story to correct minutiae such as, 'No, I tell a lie, it wasn't a Monday, it was a Tuesday'. They'll even qualify it with, 'I know it was a Tuesday because Auntie Ethel always drops in on a Tuesday'.

Q: NOW WHAT WAS THIS ABOUT FLUFFY DICE?

A: Like trainspotting, fluffy dice are a peculiarly British mystery. They are dice made of cloth with a shaggy, fleecy surface and are suspended from a car's rear view mirror. *What for?* No-one knows – this weirdest of fashions began about 30 years ago. Some people may have an effigy of a deity, or a football pennant for

3

Roma or Barcelona, and Christians might display St Christopher. These are all understandable as showing some allegiance to a faith or a team, but fluffy dice: a mystery; a uniquely British mystery akin to the mock zebra and tiger skin seat covers which despoil otherwise quite attractive car upholstery.

Q: DO THE BRITISH STILL HUNT FOXES?

A: Yes, is the short answer — the pro-hunt and anti-hunt lobby have been at loggerheads for generations. As a recreation it evokes more passion than any other. *Why so?* On the face of it the Anti's deplore the cruelty of chasing an animal to exhaustion with the ultimate objective of allowing the hounds tear it to pieces. The Pro's argue is that the hunt is part of Britain's heritage and that the country is awash with representations of the hunt: in pub names, place mats, pictures, and memorabilia. They also claim that the hunt keeps many rural communities in work as blacksmiths, kennel workers, grooms, feed providers and all the jobs associated with the hunt. They tend to play down the cruelty factor, stressing that most foxes escape and those caught are killed within seconds. Other rather weak defences are that the fox is a cruel brute who will destroy an entire coop of chickens and that hunting keeps the numbers down.

You say 'on the face of it'? Well, like so many aspects of British life, that old bogey, class, rears its ugly head. Hunting is seen by many as a hangover from the days of a domineering aristocracy who galloped through the countryside attired in their finery. Indeed, logically it had to be the pursuit of the landed gentry and those who could afford to maintain stables and kennels, who also had the leisure time for such diversions. There always has been a certain snobbery attached to riding with hounds. So, while many of the anti-hunt lobby are genuine animal lovers who are outraged at the cruelty, others loathe the concept, as they see it, of the rich and privileged flaunting their socially superior pastimes in the face of rural communities living on low incomes. *So it's more to do with people than foxes?* You could say that.

Q: WHO IS GOING TO WIN, THE PRO'S OR THE ANTI'S?

A: On 13 February 2002 a bill was passed by the Scottish Parliament banning the hunt. Because of the popular bias against hunting, the bill was a rather rushed affair with 107 amendments. It lacked coherence, was badly constructed and, although the issue may be considered dead by some, it looks as though it won't lie down. A similar bill was then passed in the

Westminster UK parliament on 18 March (384 against, 175 for). The pro lobby is very strong. Many of them resent the idea of townspeople who know nothing of their country ways bossing country people about. On 21 September 2002 in London 400,000 people turned out to, as they called it, preserve their way of life. It is hard to believe the anti lobby could muster such passionate commitment.

Most fair-minded people are conscious of the sub-plots and hypocrisy in both arguments. *Such as?* The class war sub-plot mainly; for example, hare coursing was at least as brutal as is rabbit hunting with the use of terriers, but neither attracted the same opprobrium. Many argue that dragging a fish from the water with a barbed hook is cruel but none of these pursuits have the same class connotations as fox hunting. Anyone who has seen the pitiful conditions of battery-farmed pigs or chickens might wonder about distorted priorities. Others would argue that a ban on boxing is more urgent as the object of that sport is to inflict physical damage to your opponent and the ultimate accolade is a 'knock-out' which is quite literally another word for brain damage.

Q: BUT YOU CAN'T DENY BLOOD SPORTS ARE CRUEL?

A :No, but many people feel that in terms of relative importance, the issue is given too much prominence. A measure of the class war sub-plots is the disproportionate effort put into the debates. In the entire 80,000km^2 of Scotland there are only ten hunts, the largest of which is the Berwickshire, near the Border. Literally thousands of hours of parliamentary time have been devoted to the issue. The 18 March debate in Westminster took up five solid hours of parliamentary time and one can tell from the result that 559 members voted – in other words the 'House was packed'.

The irony is that the vast majority of the British public have never seen a fox hunt nor listened to the toot of the huntsman's horn, let alone heard the idiotic cry of 'Tally-ho'. Our legislators will decide but, relative to vital matters such as nuclear weapons, the old age pension, the Health Service, unemployment and drugs, it really is a trivial issue. A hundred times more foxes are slaughtered on our roads by motorists than by foxhounds yet when the case for a ban is raised in parliament, MPs and MSPs queue up to deliver passionate oratory for both sides of the argument. To give a clearer perspective, the number of MPs attending the fox hunting debates has been comparable to the numbers attending debates as to whether Tony Blair should have supported George W Bush in military action against Iraq.

5

Q: WE SAW ON BRITISH TV THAT FOX HUNTING STILL GOES ON?

A: Yes, it is only the means of despatch of the fox which has changed. The fox may be pursued as before but now a marksman with a rifle will kill the fox before the hounds can tear it to pieces.

Q: WHAT ARE THE MOST POPULAR SPORTS IN SCOTLAND?

A: Using TV viewing as a benchmark, football (soccer) is number one and snooker is second. Fishing is the major participation (as opposed to viewing) sport in the UK. After football, golf is the number two activity in Scotland but not quite so high up the scale in England. *Why so?* Hard to say really. Some sports are associated much more with England than Scotland, such as cricket, croquet, tennis, polo, Rugby, squash and badminton. There were class affiliations with some games. In fact, the reason England produced so many games was because the gentlemen and ladies of yester-year by definition did no work and consequently needed as many diversions as possible to occupy their under-employed bodies. In Scotland the weather has been a deciding factor in the recreations we take part in.

Q: WHAT'S A MUNRO AND HOW DO YOU BAG ONE?

A: A Munro is any Scottish mountain over 3000ft, roughly 914m. They are named after Sir H T Munro who, in 1891, made the first formal listing of them. He recorded the total number of peaks at 3000ft plus, as 279. As more precise measuring methods evolved some were promoted and some demoted but the figure as recognized by the Scottish Mountaineering Club is now 284. To bag one is to climb one.

Q: ANY MUNRO YOU WOULD RECOMMEND?

A: Unless it is important to you to claim you have climbed a Munro, the answer is no. There are countless hills throughout Scotland under the 914m threshold which provide stunning views and an exhilarating day's climbing. No scenic trip is Scotland is complete without a visit to the Trossachs, sometimes called 'The Highlands in Miniature'. While you're there, try Ben Ledi at 876m or Ben Venue at 729m. The views over the Trossachs and Loch Katrine will take your breath away. If you are heading further north up the

A82 past Loch Lomond, Ben Vorlich at 942m is well worth the climb. North of Loch Lomond you are spoiled for choice. If you're in the Borders try the Moffat or Galloway Hills, all below 914m.

Q: IS GOLF PRETTY BIG ALL OVER THE UK?

A: Yes, because it can be played all year round golf is hugely popular. Probably because of its Scottish origins, it is more popular north of the Border. You may freely use terms such as bogey, birdie or eagle in any Scottish pub with the ease of saying deep-fine-leg in Surrey. *Deep-fine-leg?* I'll get to this in a moment. Some say golf suits the Scots stoical character. Even the Sabbath day observers didn't see golf as abandoning oneself to enjoyment. The game can be maddeningly frustrating. It demands a great amount of concentration and consistency. Also, with a mere fraction of over-confidence the consequences can be disastrous. Just the game for a nation of philosophers, engineers and disciplined thinkers. Divine retribution lives on in a land where if the weather is too nice, someone is bound to say, 'Aye, but we'll pay for it later.'

Q: IS THAT WHY SCOTTISH GOLF COURSES ARE SO GLOOMY?

A: Gloomy! Good grief. Gloomy indeed! *What about St Andrews and Muirfield?* Oh dear, I can hear club house gin and tonics being choked upon now, but maybe you have a point. We have always tended to assume that antiquity and a level of reverence were enough to keep us in the world No 1 spot but a number of people have commented that the last Open held at Muirfield *was* the last word in dreariness. Okay there were no flowers, no shrubs, no trees, no ornamental ponds, no bunting and no apparent effort to create a sense of occasion for an international audience. We have tended to rely on our history, elitism and snobberies with elaborate blazer badges and long-discarded and pretentious military titles for club officials.

But even the holes were dull. You must remember we are not here to enjoy ourselves. Long monotonous fairways flanked by unsightly straggly grass and punishing bunkers are the Scottish way. They're rather like a paradigm for our Calvinist heritage. Calvin would have approved of Tiger Woods. Don't wander off the straight and narrow, keep to the middle of the fairway. Be disciplined and diligent and you can achieve paradise (aka a birdie). Take risks or have a tantrum like Colin Montgomerie and you are doomed, utterly doomed. *Frankly, we thought St Andrews was even more boring!* Now that is blasphemous!

Why? It was like a flat monotonous walk by the sea.

But what about the Old Course, The Royal and Ancient, the Swilken Bridge, the history, the memories, the atmosphere!

Easy. I like to enjoy my golf. I don't want to feel like a pilgrim.

So I suppose you'd prefer the luxurious blazing colours of Augusta, the hot sunshine, the blue skies, the shorts and tee-shirts, the happy crowds, the smiles, the gaiety and all that stuff?

You bet.

Q: WHAT'S HAPPENED TO SCOTLAND'S NATIONAL SOCCER TEAM?

A: This is a question that fills countless column inches in the press. We seemed to reach a nadir when we drew with the Faeroe Islands in the Euro qualifiers. *Was this in Egypt?* No, no — not the Pharaohs, although one is tempted to draw comparisons between them and the lack of animation in our team. The Faeroes are a group of small islands up in the North Atlantic. Their national team is comprised of plumbers, policemen and others with full-time occupations.

One of the most common explanations offered for our lacklustre team is the dominance of the Old Firm, Glasgow's Celtic and Rangers (for more see Chapter 4). So much attention is focused on these teams and the partisanship is so intense that the national team can be seen almost as an after-thought. With boring predictability the two teams fill the first and second places in the Scottish Premier League year after year. Both stadia consistently attract over 50,000 fans which makes them enormously wealthy. The massive following demands success at any price. Consequently, young, aspiring Scottish players are overlooked and the foreign players in the Old Firm vastly outnumber native Scots. It is not uncommon for one of the teams to field 11 non-Scots. Millions of pounds continue to be spent on importing the best players money can buy, consequently any Scottish National team will lack experience of playing top level football.

Some say another reason for the team's demise is that the Scotland v England annual fixture was scrapped. This annual contest once galvanised support in both countries. Hampden Park would be packed to capacity and the away match at Wembley saw hordes of Scottish supporters known as The Tartan Army descend on London, wildly rooting for a win over the Auld Enemy. Even an Old Firm match could not equal the passion of Scots fans, most of whom were dressed in kilts and wrapped in Scottish colours. It was an occasion of excitement, fun and patriotic fervour where every young lad dreamed of pulling on the Scottish jersey and belting one past the English goalie. Equally important is that it took the focus off the nasty internecine hostility associated with the Old Firm fixtures. Now the England match is history and much of the fervour that once followed the national team is directed at the two big Glasgow teams.

Q: SO HOW COME THE IRISH SOCCER TEAM DOES SO WELL?

A: Probably because there is no down-side. There is no football league of any significance in Ireland. Soccer is still a bit of a Johnny-come-lately sport, so if the national side gets to compete in any major competition, people are delighted. Any win is a joy and losing merits no shame. An English loss is considered a national disaster. The Irish will party, win or lose. This was borne out in the 2002 World Cup. The returning Irish team received a rapturous welcome in Dublin and a massive celebratory party in the Phoenix Park. The English team who went a stage further than the Irish came home to a very subdued reception.

Q: WHAT ABOUT RUGBY?

A: Very popular in some areas, less so in others. In Scotland it is very big in the Borders area and the East, much less so in the West where football dominates. Though the game originated at Rugby private school in England, it enjoyed huge, across-the-board appeal in Wales. In the industrial North of England it re-emerged as Rugby League, a faster more visually entertaining game where the League Cup invariably goes home to Lancaster or Yorkshire. *Why the Rugby/Soccer divide?* It is not a huge divide but the Scottish Borders region produces a great number of big-boned, broad men from the predominantly farming community. These horny-handed sons of the soil were better designed for the crunching contacts made in rugby while urban Lanarkshire produced more lean and wiry men whose nimbleness could be applied to great effect on the soccer field. Also, the east coast of Scotland has a proportionately higher number of private schools where the preferred game was, and still is, rugby. Having said that, the top team in Scotland is currently Glasgow Hawks!

Q: AND CRICKET?

A: Never big in Scotland, Ireland and Wales but is very popular in England. Britain's premier serious radio station, Radio 4, can devote days to the game. For hours at a time, the slowest ball game in history — on the radio. Even on TV, cricket won't make too many pulses race, but radio! Clearly the enthusiasts derive great pleasure from the coverage but for those unfamiliar with the game, it has the complexity of a Masonic rite. Commentaries are awash with references to deep-fine-leg, googlies, leg-side, off-side, overs, off-spinners, leg-spinners, all out before tea, LBW, maidens, off-stumps, seam-bowlers and more arcane terms than you could shake a stick at. Many non-aficionados, who have not acquired the language, love the game purely for its image. There is something tremendously soothing about a village green dotted with men in white, not doing anything very energetic apart from the occasional whack of leather on willow and a brief dash from one wicket to the other. The sound of polite clapping rippling round the perimeter of the green from retired men in straw hats while womenfolk in summer frocks pour tea and dispense neatly cut sandwiches, provides a balm for stress-ridden souls.

Q: HOW BIG IS CURLING?

A: Curling is a minority sport. One factor which stunted its growth was global warming. For roughly 500 years, since the sport began with monks from Paisley Abbey sliding lumps of granite at a target, Scottish winters have been cold enough for lochs to freeze to a sufficient density to allow curling. When the ice was thick enough, about 8 inches (20cm), a 'Bonspiel' or 'Great Match' would be held and curlers from miles around would gather at a central loch for a day of curling. The Lake of Menteith was always a main venue. *Lake not Loch?* Yes, the only lake in Scotland. The story goes that the surrounding land was know as the Laich of Menteith, Laich being the old Scots word for low-lying land or a flat plateau. The area around the water is quite flat and it is said that when Anglophone cartographers were first producing detailed maps of the area they misheard laich as lake. Since the advent of global warming, in the last 50 years the Lake of Menteith has only once (1979) frozen to a safe density so the opportunity for mass enjoyment of the game has not existed. There are several curling rinks around Scotland but they can only accommodate the dedicated few.

It will be interesting to see how curling develops now that Scotland, sorry, Britain won the Gold Medal in the female curling event at Salt Lake City's Winter Olympics. Although very much a minority sport, some eight million Britons watched the curling final and both the Prime Minister and the Prince of Wales sent messages of congratulation to the winners. Prince Charles alluded cryptically to the women's achievement in this 'ancient Scottish sport', which just may have been a gentle hint that he was fully aware that this 'British' victory was very much a Scottish affair. Another team of Scots ladies won the World Championship (this time for Scotland!) almost straight after the Olympics.

Q: WHERE ARE THE BEST PLACES TO SWIM?

A: The short answer is that in Scotland you are wisest to stick to the Solway Coast or the West Coast. The Gulf Stream (North Atlantic Drift) maintains a moderate temperature on these coasts. Even up as far as the Outer Hebrides (further north than Latvia) the sea temperature is tolerable enough to permit a swim. The eastern seaboard of the North Sea is influenced more by the Norwegian Sea and the waters further north. On the hottest day on the wonderful West Sands at St Andrews (where the opening scenes of Chariots of Fire were filmed), you can see the bravest and strongest run enthusiastically across the sand to the inviting blue sea. With the submersion of just one toe, the runner loses all acceleration and by the time both ankles are immersed the would-be swimmer is seriously considering abandoning the idea; the only dilemma being how to effect a retreat without one's loved ones jeering 'chicken' as they soak up the sun's rays. The hot days are actually the worst as the difference between ambient temperature and sea temperature is the greatest.

With freshwater lochs, in summer, the smaller and shallower the loch the higher the temperature as the sun has a chance to penetrate the water. River bathing is only for the brave.

Q: WHAT DOES THE AVERAGE ADULT DO FOR RECREATION?

A: Very little, as Scotland's Health Education Board (HEB) figures will confirm. The single greatest occupier of spare time is watching TV.

In fairness, there is no credit to the beautiful people of Southern California jogging on a balmy evening to the sound of the Pacific lapping on a sandy beach. It takes a real act of will to don even a warm track suit and venture into a dark, rainy Auchtermuchty evening with a cold, wet wind cutting at your face like barbed wire. To complement such a self-flagellating fitness routine with a salad garnished with low fat mayonnaise is the stuff of which monastic life is made. In these latitudes, a choice between the healthy lifestyle and a steaming hot steak pie in a pool of thick gravy with deep fried chips and onions is no contest. And if this heart-warning meal is preceded by a session in a smoky pub and followed by a glass or two of Scotland's national drink the appeal is overwhelming.

But people can't live like that. They don't. Scotland has one of the highest premature death rates in the affluent world and Lanarkshire (in the former Strathclyde Region) has the highest in Scotland. The big killers are heart attacks, cancer and strokes. In

March 2003 the Public Health Institute for Scotland commissioned a survey on longevity for women. Of the 25 countries listed the top five were Japan, France, Switzerland, Italy and Spain and bottom of the list — Scotland. It's a multi-factorial problem but part of it is attitude. The West of Scotland experienced a massive decline in all the industries that once made Glasgow the Second City of the Empire. Coal, steel, shipbuilding and textiles have all gone, generating, in some quarters, a feeling of defeat. Smoking, bad diet and lack of exercise are therefore not the major concerns they would be to a prosperous middle-class. It's not just fiscal poverty: it is, to use the phrase of Scottish Socialist Party leader, Tommy Sheridan, a 'poverty of aspiration'.

What's the answer? If there was an easy answer, the statistics of early death would be in decline, however, we know it can be done. For years Finland used to compete neck-and-neck with Scotland in the early-death league but a massive education campaign in Finland on the risks of high cholesterol food, smoking, lack of exercise and over-consumption of vodka, managed to bring Finland's bad record more in line with healthy Norway and Sweden.

Can't Scotland copy Finland? No reason why not and it appears the Scottish Parliament is taking the problem seriously. Some of the HEB TV adverts aimed at the young, portraying smoking and excessive drinking as uncool may well help the growing generation break the habits of old. One problem is peer-group pressure and its counterpart peer-group reassurance. The middle-class guest who produces a cigarette packet after dinner is looked upon with disdain, increasing the pressure on smokers to give up. The reverse applies lower down the social scale. In many groups of workers the majority will smoke, thus reducing pressure to stop and providing the reassurance to continue.

Q: IF TV IS SUCH A MAJOR RECREATION, IT MUST BE PRETTY GOOD?

A: From a world perspective, British TV is excellent. The BBC's original charter was to Educate, Inform and Entertain and on the whole it continues to do this, setting the benchmark for the commercial channels. The quality of programmes on wildlife, documentaries, history, investigative journalism and other non-fiction subjects is consistently high. Sure there is fodder for the brain-dead — game shows, soaps, quiz shows and the ubiquitous reality 'get-me-out-of-here' shows, but all nations seem to descend to this lowest common denominator of entertainment. To see the noble Spanish throwing custard pies at each other in some inane game show or the inscrutable Japanese, who lay so much store in restraint and pride, squealing in horror as they do unspeakable things to one another in the name of TV fun, reassures us that we are not the worst. Oddly, at a time when the BBC has been accused of dumbing down, the demand for history programmes continues to grow.

Q: Do you still pay a licence fee to watch TV?

A: We do and though some resent paying it, there is little doubt that it prevents all TV channels descending into a ratings war. Time is allocated to religious broadcasting, Gaelic language and other minority interest subjects that wouldn't stand a chance in a commercial free-for-all ratings war. Our commercial channels in Scotland, Scottish Television, Grampian and Borders tend to follow the benchmark set by the BBC. Regrettably, they are all moving targets for the commercial big boys who view them merely as takeover opportunities for advertising revenue.

CHAPTER 2
POLITICS, HISTORY
AND CULTURAL IDENTITY

Q: How accurate was the movie Braveheart?

A: Braveheart was a movie phenomenon. It focused on a rather obscure period of Scottish history which has always played second fiddle to English/British history, yet people from all over the world have seen the movie and expressed interest in it. *Like where?* Naturally the biggest market was the English-speaking world of North America, Australia, New Zealand and South Africa. As regards accuracy, a lot of history purists were very critical and dismissive of the movie. Sure there were some liberties taken with the facts but, relative to Errol Flynn winning WWII single-handed or Messrs Wayne and Stallone re-writing the history of the Vietnam war, this movie was a fair representation of the truth.

Q: So how much of the movie was made-up?

A: The basics were all pretty correct. There were a few Hollywood liberties taken such as the on-screen affair between Wallace and Edward's French wife, Isabella of Angouleme. When Wallace was put to death in 1305, Isabella was only seven years old, but movies are seldom made with an academic audience in mind and the love interest did add to the enjoyment. On a point of history, it is fair to record that Isabella was predisposed to take a lover in view of her husband's disinterest in that particular department. Her lover, Roger Mortimer, virtually ruled England once Edward II had been deposed.

Q: What exactly is the story?

A: Scotland had no king after the death of Alexander III in 1286. His heir was his infant grand-daughter, The Maid of Norway. The Maid's great uncle, Edward of England, arranged to marry her to his son. This would have united the Scottish and English crowns but the Maid fell ill on the sea journey and died, leaving Scotland without an obvious ruler. About a dozen nobles squabbled as to who should succeed. The front runners as claimants were Robert de Brus (the Bruce) and John Balliol, the latter having the strongest claim. They asked Edward I of England (allegedly the greatest lawyer of his time) to referee but Edward wanted to know what was in it for him so invoked the long disputed and tenuous claim that any Scottish king should be subordinate to the English king. The Scottish aristocracy, who always placed their sectional interests above the best interests of Scotland, agreed, declared for Balliol and duly paid homage to Edward. This was accurately represented in the movie.

Edward 'Longshanks' was tall and imposing and was aged 66 when he first stormed Berwick. Patrick McGoohan was perfectly cast as Edward. Wallace was some 40 years the junior of Edward which came across as quite convincing in the movie. Wallace was 35 when brutally executed in London. Again, quite convincing.

Q: IF THE SCOTS NOBLES ACCEPTED EDWARD AS THE BIG CHIEF, WHY WASN'T THERE PEACE?

A: It was when Edward (as Lord Superior) demanded Scottish help in his war against France that the Scots magnates rebelled and formed an alliance with the French (October 1295). Edward was none too happy about this and invaded Scotland a year later where he deposed Balliol. The aristocracy (as is their wont) submitted to Edward by signing and sealing The Ragman Roll. The consequent resentment of the people was harnessed by William 'Braveheart' Wallace and Andrew Moray who defeated Edward at Stirling Bridge and swept the English from Scotland. All pretty accurately conveyed in the movie. Edward's son was portrayed clearly with homosexual preferences; this is quite factual and was the cause of the particularly brutal method of his murder. The favourite of Edward II was Piers Gaveston who, in the movie, was thrown out of a window by Edward I but was in fact lynched on the orders of Thomas of Lancaster. What was so accurate was Edward Senior's loathing of his son's lifestyle. The manner of Gaveston's death was not germane to the story.

Q: WASN'T GIBSON A LOT OLDER THAN WALLACE?

A: Mel Gibson looked older than Wallace (who was only 27 at Stirling Bridge) and Wallace was a lot taller than Gibson — even the movie chose to make a joke at Gibson's expense on this issue. ('That cannae be Wallace, he's no tall enough'). Other historic details were adapted to fit a two-hour movie but, all in all, it is a quite reasonable representation of a very interesting chapter of Scottish history.

Q: WHY WAS THE MOVIE BRAVEHEART SO POPULAR?

A: Firstly, it was a damn good movie with McGoohan as a formidable Edward and Gibson an excellent Wallace; even his Scottish accent was quite passable. But it really struck a chord in countries where there is huge interest in Scottish heritage, such as Canada, the USA, the Antipodes and South Africa.

There was also the Irish dimension as much of it was filmed in Ireland with the Irish Army filling the ranks of both the English and Scottish warriors – though it is rumoured the bulk of the extras volunteered to 'fight' on the Scottish side. So the movie had widespread popular appeal. Perhaps more importantly, it was a hugely popular movie in Scotland. **Why?** Well, apart from the entertainment value of the movie, there has always been a policy of teaching British history in Scottish Schools. British history tended to focus mostly on English history — 1066 and all that. More of their own history is now being taught to Scottish kids but many Scots adults who saw the movie declared they knew hardly anything about the Scottish Wars of Independence until they saw Braveheart.

Q: WAS MARY QUEEN OF SCOTS 'BLOODY MARY'?

A: No; Bloody Mary was Queen of England (1553-8), the first queen to rule England in her own right. The Scottish Mary reigned from 1542 to 1567. Bloody Mary acquired the nickname from the persecution of Protestants during her reign, which saw almost 300 burned at the stake. She was unlikely to look too kindly on the new religion as her mother was Catherine of Aragon whom Henry VIII had divorced (see p 87 on Religion).

Q: WHY IS MARY QUEEN OF SCOTS SO FAMOUS?

A: Because of her wild, romantic, impulsive life and her extraordinary death. She was just six days old when she became Queen; as a child she was promised in marriage to Henry VIII's weakling son Edward; at six years of age she was spirited away to France to escape the union with Edward and married the heir to the French throne, Francis, at 15 (he was 14). She became Queen of France at 17 and was widowed at 18 in 1560, the same year her mother died. She returned to Scotland at age 19. At 23 she remarried, unwisely. Her new husband was her cousin — the worthless Darnley. Her favourite courtier and fancy-man – **Fancy-man?** – sorry, Scots colloquialism for a lover or a 'bit on the side'

— a chap called Riccio, was then murdered with her husband's involvement. In the same year she gave birth to the future James VI. Shortly afterwards, when Mary was 25, her husband was murdered. Mary is believed to have been involved in Darnley's murder as by this time she was the lover of Bothwell whom she married later.

By this time Scotland had had enough turmoil and she was forced to abdicate. She was imprisoned in a castle in the middle of Loch Leven in Fife but escaped in 1568, aged 26, and finally, after a failed attempt to reclaim the throne, fled to England to seek refuge with her cousin Queen Elizabeth. Mary, being a Catholic and Elizabeth's nearest relative, was viewed with suspicion by the English and Mary was imprisoned. Continued talk of Mary's plotting to take the English throne led to her execution at Fotheringay Castle in 1587 at the relatively young age of 45. She died with great dignity, redeeming herself in the eyes of posterity.

Her tempestuous life along with her good looks and great vivacity gave her a most prominent place in history. Whether Elizabeth's mind had been poisoned by her spies or whether she was the primary force behind Mary's execution is uncertain. Some historians say Elizabeth felt profound remorse after her cousin's death.

Q: HOW LEGITIMATE WAS MARY'S CLAIM TO THE ENGLISH THRONE?

A: Her claim was based on the fact that her grandmother, Margaret Tudor, was the sister of Henry VIII. There were those who did not recognise Henry's divorce from Catherine of Aragon and therefore Elizabeth, the daughter of his second wife, Anne Boleyn, was illegitimate. Though Mary acknowledged that Elizabeth was rightful ruler of England, Elizabeth never forgot that Mary had once claimed her throne.

Q: WHY DIDN'T MARY FLEE TO FRANCE?

A very good question. Her first language was French. She was always happiest in France; she loved the refinement of the French court, the better climate and the way of life which was one of the reasons she was drawn to the polished Riccio. She had family in France along with some land. She could have lived a very comfortable life in the country where she was once queen. Some say her flight to England was evidence of her interest in the English throne. We can't be sure.

Q: WAS MACBETH FOR REAL?

A: Yes indeed, though Shakespeare's Scottish Play has often meant that the eponymous character be considered fictional. Macbeth was king of Scotland (Alba) from 1040 to 1057. He was Mormaer or The Great Steward of Moray (a province of Alba) and the grandson of Malcolm II. Macbeth killed his cousin Duncan I in battle, made a pilgrimage to Rome and was eventually defeated by Malcolm Canmore, not at Dunsinane but near Lumphanan, Aberdeenshire.

Why is Macbeth **referred to as 'the Scottish Play' by actors?**

Oh, it's a bit of theatrical nonsense really. Actors, like sailors, are said to be full of superstitions and the thespian world is awash with stories of disasters that have befallen performances of Macbeth. The use of the name was said to herald bad luck, hence the adoption of the alternative title.

And Brigadoon?

Entirely fictional. The appalling film set was fictional as well because after the director Vincente Minnelli had toured Scotland trying in vain to find a suitable location for the village, he gave up claiming that, 'I came to find Brigadoon, but I couldn't find it anywhere', or words to that effect!

Q: HOW BIG A MASSACRE WAS GLENCOE?

A: On the Scottish history slaughter-scale the number of people murdered was not great. At dawn on the eve of St Valentine's Day 1692, 38 Macdonalds were killed by the Campbells, but it was not so much the scale as the circumstances.

To put it in a historical context, James VII (James II of Great Britain) had converted to Catholicism. The birth of his son in 1688 and the possibility of a Catholic succession made James the personification of the 'Popish Threat'. After James, the nearest in line to the throne was Mary, wife of William of Orange. This led leading statesmen to invite William and Mary to take the British throne. With two claimants, something had to give. The deciding contest was at the Battle of the Boyne in 1690. The Catholic James VII and II was defeated by the Protestant William of Orange. The new regime of William and Mary, which replaced the Stewarts, required the wild and fiercely independent Highland chiefs to swear allegiance to their majesties. Among the chiefs who were more reluctant than others was Alexander Macdonald, or Maclain of Glencoe. An oath had to be signed in front of a magistrate before 1 Jan 1692 so the stubborn Maclain plodded off to Fort William the day before the deadline only to be told that the nearest magistrate was in Inveraray. Although Maclain did sign up after the deadline, it was decided that to show who was boss an example was to be made of the Macdonalds. Using the tried and tested formula of divide and rule, the Campbells were brought in to do the dirty work. Although old adversaries, the Campbells were fellow Highlanders and when they approached the MacDonalds seeking hospitality, the Macdonalds felt obliged to extend the necessary accommodation.

During the Campbell's 12-day stay, many of the Macdonalds expressed serious concern about the strangers in their midst. Maclain ruled that Highland hospitality was inviolable and no guest could be harassed. The breaking of bread together had an almost biblical symbolism. Just before dawn on 13 Feb the Campbells and other Redcoats struck, killing men, women and children. People were bayoneted in their beds and houses were torched as the massacre progressed. Such butchery of the unarmed and unprepared would have found a special place in the annals of notoriety, but for guests to inflict such brutality on their hosts was to the Highlander, a crime crying out to heaven for divine retribution. In fairness, the Campbells were only the spearhead of government action and it is said that some of the Campbells tried to warn the Macdonald victims while others fired wide of their targets, so there appears to be areas of grey in this otherwise starkly black and white picture.

Q: DOES THE MEMORY OF GLENCOE STILL BURN?

A: Certainly such an act will never be forgotten and there will still be Macdonalds who might only consider supping with a Campbell using a long spoon. Interestingly in March 2002, the National Trust for Scotland appointed a new manager for the Glencoe Visitor Centre — his name: Roddy Campbell. In Glencoe the appointment was viewed with more wry humour than any sense of outrage.

Q: THE SCOTS DON'T LIKE BEING CALLED ENGLISH, DO THEY?

A: No they don't, but to put the question in the clearest perspective, you have to reverse it. If you said to an Englishman, 'You're Scottish aren't you?' He would reply 'No I'm not, I'm English and proud of it'. Quite right too. But somehow the denial is seen as more acceptable from the Englishman – the Scots tend to be labelled brittle or touchy if they assert their nationality.

Explain! It's all a matter of perception really. The Scots see themselves first as Scottish and their country, with all its traditions, is very much their home. England to the Scot, particularly the further south he goes, seems alien to him. But Scotland has a population of only five million, some two million short of London's population, so the English seldom think of Scotland. While Scotland is awash with English newspapers, TV and radio shows, hardly anyone in the deep south has ever heard of the *Herald* or the *Scotsman* or would tune in to BBC Radio Scotland (if they could). The main news programmes are broadcast from London with a local or 'regional' five-minute attachment at the end.

English visitors in Scotland will not hesitate to order 'a full English breakfast', and should the staff respond, 'I can do you a full Scottish breakfast,' then the English will say, 'Oh, you know what I mean'. Or, during some particularly extreme weather you can hear, 'one doesn't expect these conditions in England, does one'. The reply, 'Actually you are in Scotland' will only evoke another, 'Oh, you know what I mean.' Recently at Barcelona airport I witnessed a slightly agitated Englishman who clearly needed some information dashing up to a pale-looking couple and saying 'You're English aren't you?' The man replied, 'No, I'm Irish and my wife is from Wales.' The response – wait for it – was a mildly irritated, 'Yes, yes ... but you know what I mean!'

Q: SO THE ENGLISH LIKE PUTTING THE SCOTS DOWN?

A: Not really. The English mean no offence whatever. Paradoxically, it is often their very unawareness that upsets the Scots so much. It is all a matter of demographics — like an hourglass, the sand is all in the bottom. (See also the Scottish Parliament question on page 23). This exists on mainland Europe where continentals will freely say, 'You are Engleesh, no?' to Scots, Irish and Welsh alike. However, the countless references to England instead of Britain do irritate the Scots. Here are just a few of many examples of statements made after the 1707 Act of Union:

England expects that every man will do his duty — Nelson
The defence of England — Stanley Baldwin
England is the mother of parliaments — John Bright
1940, when England stood alone — almost everyone
England is only a little island — Eric Linklater
England mourns for her dead — Binyon (*Poems for the Fallen*)
Wake up England — King George V
The Queen of England — almost everyone, especially Americans!
Who do you think you are kidding Mr Hitler, if you think old England's done — opening line from the signature tune to Dad's Army (popular 1970s TV programme about the Home Guard).

The numbering of British monarchs is irritatingly anglocentric. It began with William IV who should have been William I of Britain. Victoria's wastrel son Edward should have been Edward I of Britain and not Edward VII and Elizabeth II should be Elizabeth I of Britain.

Q: IS THIS SCOTTISH/BRITISH DISTINCTION IMPORTANT?

A: You'll find a fuller answer in the next chapter. It shouldn't be important but many Scots have felt like the poor relation ever since the Act of Union in 1707. Scots think like a nation and have many of the symbols of nationhood such as Scottish law, the Church, the Saltire, rugby team, football team and others but, in the Olympics, Scotland competes as part of Great Britain. There is a fixed idea in Scotland (unfortunately with quite a degree of evidence) that when Scots athletes win something, the UK commentators describe the victory as British but when they lose they are all too often Scottish. It happened in the 2002 Winter Olympics when the British women's curling team, who had performed quite well, looked as though they were going to be knocked out at the semi-final stage and an English TV commentator actually said, 'It looks like they are turning a British victory into a Scottish disaster.' A rather confused statement but hurtful nonetheless. Also, because there are virtually no English curlers, sections of the English press chose to poke fun at this alien sport, one even alluding to 'Scottish scrubbers'. The team came in for some barbed criticism from no less a paper than *The Times* describing them as 'looking like electricians' wives'. This may seem incomprehensible to honest American minds but in a British context it does rather encapsulate the patronising attitude of the South towards the North.

Q: SO THE SCOTS ARE A BIT TOUCHY ABOUT THIS?

A: Yes, no getting away from it. Of course it happens all over the world. Some Europeans make fun of the Belgians and the Belgians themselves have internecine friction between the French speakers and the Dutch speakers. Northern Irish Unionists can be touchy about being called Irish. Canadians don't like being called Americans. Canada however, is a large prosperous, independent nation with a clear national identity. Five million Scots can feel more like an adjunct to a powerful and dominant nation of fifty-five million people. The Scottish broadcaster Ludovic Kennedy, who has plied his trade mainly south of the Border, covered this subject in his book *In Bed with an Elephant* in 1995. The touchiness is more emotional than rational. One Scottish

Nationalist MSP suggested that the Scots should grow up and have the independence of mind and strength of character to support England in the 2003 Rugby World Cup after the Scottish team had been knocked out. Rationally all Scots agreed but emotionally the argument was dead in the water. Even when the English soccer team runs out onto the pitch to play against Turkey, Tanzania or Tajikistan (it matters not), Scots find an incomprehensible and overwhelming allegiance to nations east of The Aegean.

Q: But you are such a small island, it doesn't make sense.

A: True, to an objective observer it does seem crazy but Ireland is also a small island, so is Cyprus, as is Sri Lanka, and they live with even greater divisions. Sometimes, in the human psyche, the emotional and the rational are irreconcilable. The English intellectual acceptance of being a second-rate power and the enfant terrible of Europe is often at odds with the emotions evoked by Harfleur, Creçy, Drake, Nelson, Wellington, Dunkirk and the 1966 World Cup. Similarly with the Scots; they work with the English, drink with them and even marry them, but somewhere in the deep recesses of the Celtic soul there are echoes of Bannockburn, Falkirk and Stirling Bridge. There are confused memories of the Penal Laws after the 1746 Battle of Culloden, Prestonpans, the Highland Clearances and the thousand and one slights from being the very junior partner in an arranged union.

Most Scots agree that it is rational to support England on the sports field but an example of the heart-versus-head dichotomy was on an east-coast train on the day of the England v Brazil quarter-final match in the 2002 World Cup. Though the train started off from York, it picked up over 300 Scots at Dunbar who were commuting to Edinburgh. Somewhere between Dunbar and Edinburgh, the English guard cheerfully announced that England had scored and now led Brazil 1-0. The silence was deafening.

Q: Aren't the Scots being a bit over-sensitive?

A: You're doing it now. Okay, from an English perspective it may seem a bit pernickety and as the English outnumber Scots by ten to one, their perception will be the dominant one. But if you are brought up in Scotland you see the United Kingdom from a subjective view. None of these references to Britain as England work both ways. There is an ingrained assumption in the south that English and British are synonyms, as in ex-Prime Minister John Major's reference to 'a thousand years of British history.' (Great Britain has only been around since 1707). 'Yes, yes, but you know what I mean.' It is the insistence that those north of the border should know what the others mean that can make the Scot just a wee bit tetchy.

On the face of it, it might seem somewhat petty to our visitors from the big world and for that matter from England. However, no-one would even consider placing Ireland as part of England or ordering 'a full English breakfast' in Co Kerry.

Q: WHAT'S THE DIFFERENCE BETWEEN THE SALTIRE AND THE LION RAMPANT?

A: Though both are waved with equal vigour at sporting events the blue Saltire with the white cross of St Andrew is Scotland's national flag. The Lion Rampant is the flag of the Scottish monarch.

Q: SCOTLAND NOW HAS IT'S OWN PARLIAMENT, CORRECT?

A: Yes, after the Act of Union of 1707 the Scottish Parliament was dissolved. All members of parliament thereafter had to attend the Houses of Parliament at Westminster. The Scottish desire for its own parliament has waxed and waned but never died. After a decisive referendum on 11 September 1997, the Scottish Parliament reconvened on 9 July 1999.

Q: WHAT EFFECT HAS THE SCOTTISH PARLIAMENT HAD?

A: Materially very little. Daily living has undergone no significant change apart perhaps from further increases in Edinburgh property prices, but psychologically Scots feel better about themselves and, whether people are aware of it or not, focus has shifted almost entirely from London to Edinburgh. Being a small country we all know our MSPs or know someone who does. We know where they live, which schools and universities they attended, the pubs they drank in, their lovers, their spouses, their football allegiances. Before devolution, Scottish MPs boarded trains and planes for London on a Monday and we really knew little of what they did. One interesting development is that there is a growing number of Scottish economists and academics of all political parties, and none who are coming round to the view that Scotland would be better off with total fiscal independence.

Q: HAS DEVOLUTION KILLED OFF THE MOVEMENT FOR INDEPENDENCE?

A: That was a popular belief amongst the unionist parties, particularly New Labour, but wiser counsels weren't so sure. If the Holyrood parliament is a success, then it is not unreasonable to ask that if Scotland can run its domestic affairs efficiently, why can't it run all its affairs like other small independent nations such as Ireland, Denmark, Norway, Finland etc? Also, the argument in favour of full fiscal control, whether intended or not, is a de facto argument for independence as a nation.

Q: SO HOW MUCH POWER DOES SCOTLAND'S PARLIAMENT HAVE?

A: Prior to devolution, the budget allocated by Westminster for the running of Scotland was £32 billion a year. After the establishment of a devolved government, £16 billion was transferred to Holyrood from Westminster. So in terms of simple arithmetic Scotland has a 50% control over its affairs. Conflicts of interest can arise such as Scotland's strong stance against the war in Iraq or that the majority of the people of Scotland do not want nuclear weapons on their soil yet the Westminster government sited them at Faslane, close to Scotland's densest conurbation.

Q: WHAT CAN HOLYROOD AND WESTMINSTER CONTROL?

A: Devolution sounded like Westminster handed Scotland a list of things they could control. What actually happened was Westminster decided what powers it would retain and by logical extension everything else was a devolved matter. Westminster retains control over matters which directly affect the United Kingdom as a whole, i.e. defence, foreign affairs and social security while Holyrood controls those factors which solely affect Scotland, such as health, education, finance, social justice and tourism. Nationalists argue that power devolved is power retained. *Excuse me?* It sounds contradictory doesn't it. It was a phrase coined by the late Tory politician, the scholarly Enoch Powell, who reasoned that if Party A has the power to tell Party B what it may or may not do, Party A is in effect exercising authority over B, therefore power devolved is power retained.

Q: Do Scots MPs still sit in Westminster?

A: Yes. After devolution all 72 Scots MPs retained their seats at Westminster, despite having 129 MSPs. *That's quite a lot isn't it?* Very much so; using the simple arithmetic factor above where Holyrood controls half of Scottish affairs, logically Scotland should lose half its representation in Westminster. *Will it?* No. Despite recent debates on the matter in Westminster, the figure has been set at 59 remaining out of the 72, so just 13 Scottish constituencies are to be abolished. Holyrood will retain 129 MSPs until further notice.

Q: How many Scots want independence?

A: It is very hard to quantify because pollsters tend to count the number of people voting for the Scottish National Party which fluctuates around 35 per cent of those polled, but there is also the Scottish Socialist vote and the Green Party vote who support independence. Additionally, there are a number of people who vote New Labour and Liberal Democrat (both unionist parties) who are quite sympathetic towards an independent Scotland. Demographics come into this as well. Britain fought two world wars as the United Kingdom. Many older people have strong memories of the unity of spirit in fighting a common enemy and, though patriotically Scottish, still regard the Union with fondness and nostalgia. Younger people are much more likely to be pro-independence, though much less likely to vote. There is also the old Scottish Cringe and Bluster syndrome.

Q: Is the SNP linked with the British National Party?

A: No. The BNP is a right-wing party that makes no secret of its opposition to immigration and asylum seekers. What their platform of 'Britain for the British' lacks in subtlety it makes up for in clarity. Their political fortunes fluctuate but despite the passions they can arouse they have yet to gain a single seat in parliament. Though known as the BNP, their presence in Scotland is insignificant. Their main target areas are those where the density of Asian or West Indian ethnicity is highest, as in northern England.

The SNP's raison d'être has always been an independent Scotland and its political philosophy has consistently been left of centre. Since devolution they have been the main opposition party in Scotland attracting a steady 35% of the vote.

Q: DIDN'T THE SNP LOSE SEATS IN THE 2003 SCOTTISH ELECTIONS?

A: It did, but the reasons for this are not quite clear. Some pundits say it was because of the SNP's anti-war stance. Some say the wish for independence is diminishing. However, the Scottish Socialist Party increased its number of MSPs from one to six and the Greens from one to seven — and both of these parties are vociferously anti-war and pro-independence.

Q: YOU MENTIONED THE SCOTTISH CRINGE AND BLUSTER SYNDROME?

A: It is one of the many Jekyll and Hyde aspects of the Scots character. There is a great deal to bluster about. No Scottish souvenir shop is complete without the tea towel that lists all the Scottish inventions and achievements — you know the sort of thing, Bell's telephone, Dunlop's pneumatic tyre, Simpson's chloroform, Fleming's penicillin, Baird's TV, MacAdam's road surface, the fax machine, the vacuum cleaner ... the list goes on. There are also of course the philosophers, the writers, the statesmen, the generals and the businessmen. To balance this there is the darker side, the Scottish Cringe. It probably stems from 300 years of looking south for guidance and government.

Looking South?

In March 1603 the English ran out of royals. James VI of Scotland became heir to the English throne and he legged it to England becoming the first monarch of Great Britain. Scotland lost her international identity, her head of state and head of government. The voice of authority became English. The royals, the lords, the parliamentarians all spoke the tongue of received pronunciation (received from Oxford and Cambridge). As for Gaelic, it had no place either at court or in the parliament. Worse, the Crown Act of 1616 actually proscribed the use of the Gaelic language. The James VI bible was written in standard English, so even God spoke in English. Scottishness became subordinate to Englishness. To get on in life, many Scots shed their native accent. The Scots tongue and by association the country, were perceived as second rate. Despite the bluster factor, Scots began to doubt themselves.

Q: WHY DID JAMES CHOOSE LONDON?

A: In a word, size. Removing the centre of authority from the greater to the lesser area would not have been logical but from a personal aspect, James found the English court much more

obsequious and that appealed to his vain nature. Deference is not
a Scottish characteristic.

Q: WE DON'T NOTICE THE CRINGE FACTOR

A: Good. It is on the wane but it has taken time. When Radio
Scotland was launched in the 1970s we had newsreaders who
vied with one another to sound more pukka than BBC London. It
was said that the London radio newsreaders once read the news in
dinner jackets. When BBC Scotland was launched, the main
newseader, Bill Jack, sounded as if he read the news in full colonial
governor's uniform with a plumed hat at his elbow. His colleague
Mary Marquis managed to sound grander than her name.

Now we have gone quite native with the likes of comedian Andy
Cameron who remains quite incomprehensible to anyone outside
Lanarkshire or newspaper columnist Jack McLean who sounds as
though his morning gargle is a glass of razor blades soused in
Famous Grouse. On TV the flagship London-based news
programme Newsnight has been pipped in the ratings by
Newsnight Scotland. The southern bias against regional accents
has diminished and some of London's top broadcasters are
Scottish. These include James Naughtie, Kirsty Wark, Eddie Mair,
Sarah Smith and Kirsty Young. Welsh and Irish broadcasters are
also very much in evidence.

Q: BUT SCOTS HIGH ACHIEVERS ARE EVERYWHERE!

A: True, but confidence is a fragile commodity. Too many put-
downs can blind people of their real worth. The Scots' cringe
of, ' ... we cannae govern ourselves, we're no big enough, we
haven't got the resources ... ' is considered nonsense by the
nationalists who use several illustrations such as the fact that
prominent Scots politicians include the Prime Minister Tony Blair;
the late Labour leader, John Smith (father of aforementioned
Sarah); the Chancellor of the Exchequer, Gordon Brown, Robin
Cook, ex-Leader of the House and now ex-Foreign Secretary; Tam
Dalyell, the Father of the House; Alistair Darling, Secretary of State
for the Department of Transport and Secretary of State for
Scotland; Lord Strathclyde the Leader of the Lords; Derry Irvine
the Lord Chancellor, Ian Duncan Smith, ex-Leader of the
Opposition; Charles Kennedy, the leader of the Liberal Democrats;
his predecessor David Steel; Menzies 'Ming' Campbell, Shadow
Secretary of State for Foreign & Commonwealth Affairs; Michael
Martin, the Speaker of the House and Dr John Reid, Secretary of
State for Health. The corridors of Whitehall are awash with Scottish

senior civil servants. So nationalists have a point when they scoff at the suggestion that Scotland lacks the ability for self-government.

Q: IS THIS THE NATIONALISTS' MAIN MESSAGE?

A: No, they point out that Scotland is self-sufficient in food, water and power with hydrocarbons, wind-generation and hydro-electricity in particular. A whole host of human qualities such as inventiveness, diligence, perseverance and industriousness add to the mix. The focus on the Scottish Parliament will diminish the cringe factor and may yet lead to full independence. Business in the Holyrood Parliament is conducted in natural Scots accents, even among the traditionally Anglophone Tories. However, one of the greatest obstacles to independence is a hostile Establishment.

Q: WHY IS THE ESTABLISHMENT HOSTILE TO INDEPENDENCE?

A: The entire monarchical structure is against the idea as are the vast majority of the sycophants that surround it. **Who are they all?** The royals themselves, the peers of the realm, the knights of the realm and all the countless recipients of Ruritanian gongs such as OBEs, MBEs, DBEs, CBEs etc — there are 22 varieties (almost as many as Heinz).

Q: WHAT ARE ALL THESE AWARDS AND WHY SO MANY?

A: They are relics of the zenith of the British Empire such as The Most Excellent Order of the British Empire, Dame of the British Empire and Grand Knight Commander of the Victorian Order. Then there are truly Ruritanian orders of knighthood such as Knights of the Bath, Knights of the Garter and Ladies of the Bed Chamber. To quote the late comic genius, Spike Milligan, when he was awarded the CBE he said, 'They might as well make me a Commander of Milton Keynes, at least Milton Keynes exists!'

It is quite ironic that the fictitious country Ruritania was the creation of Anthony Hope (himself a Sir), and was used to poke fun at silly foreign countries whose pomp and ritual seemed too self-important.

Q: HOW MANY PEOPLE RECEIVE THESE HONOURS?

A: Roughly 2000 people are awarded these archaic honours each year and they exercise enormous influence. There has been a long tradition of press barons — Lord Northcliffe (*Daily Mail*), his brother Lord Rothermere (*Daily Mirror*), Lord Beaverbrook, Lord Hollick, (*Daily Express*), Lord Thompson (*The Times*), Lord Deedes and, of course, Lord Conrad Black. Both of these men are involved with the *Daily Telegraph,* although Black's story is by far the most entertaining — so eager was he to sup at the alphabet soup trough ...

Alphabet soup?

It is a term of derision used to describe the twice-yearly ladling out of these endless permutations of letters which people delight in suffixing to their names. To continue ... Conrad Black was so eager to acquire a title that he renounced his Canadian citizenship to be able to call himself Lord (much to the amusement of Canadian democrats.) Alas, Black's acquisitive nature proved his downfall as he lost control of the *Daily Telegraph* over payments he made to himself of which the shareholders were unaware. He is now being sued by his former employers. There are also knights of the realm such as Sir Larry Lamb (*Sun*), Sir David English (*Daily Mail*) and the Barclay Bros (*Scotsman Publications*). The likelihood of any of these people being the tiniest bit radical is somewhat remote. The Director General of the BBC usually accepts an Establishment gong along with the standard, 'Of course I don't accept it for me but on behalf of all the loyal staff without whose dedicated efforts ... etc ... etc ... '. Except the staff can't call themselves Sir Tom, Sir Dick or Lady Harriet.

So the media is very much in the hands of the Establishment and the disproportionate level of hostility towards the Scottish Parliament is directly attributable to the Establishment status of the proprietors. The right-wing, mainly English, papers such as the *Daily Express,* the *Daily Mail* and the *Daily Telegraph* are seldom published without some disparaging comment about Holyrood and its MSPs. We also have our own home-grown anti-devolutionists including, predictably enough, those knights of the realm who own Scotsman Publications and who employ a Scottish anglophile, Andrew Neill, as editor-in-chief.

Q: WHY WOULD A SCOTTISH PAPER BE ANTI-DEVOLUTION?

A: The *Scotsman* had a long reputation for being fiercely independent and radical. It also argued for a Scottish parliament for a hundred years. Today, that once free-thinking paper is now often described as Scotland's *Daily Mail* (a pro-Establishment, conservative English daily). This influence has created great internal tension within the paper. The *Scotsman* has replaced its editor, on average, once a year ever since it adopted its more southern and anodyne journalistic style. The letters page which was once a powerhouse of trenchant and radical views now seems vapid and inconsequential. Many regular letter writers have abandoned the paper, choosing Glasgow's *Herald* for its greater breadth of topic and freedom from censorship (or editing as the *Scotsman* would have put it.)

Q: WHERE ELSE IS AFFECTED BY THE ISSUE OF TITLES AND ALPHABET SOUP?

A: The 'gong' effect can be found in a show-business parallel such as the Royal Variety Show. Over 20 minutes of this somewhat tedious show was recently devoted to a medley of pleasant but rather trite musical scores going back to the now-dated Jesus Christ Superstar. And who wrote all these uninspiring tunes? None other than the noble Lord Andrew Lloyd Webber (seated centre stalls) while the other main musical attraction was Sir Elton John. All that was missing was Sir Cliff Richard and perhaps Sir Paul McCartney. However, at the Queen's jubilee celebrations, Sir Paul joined Sir Elton and Sir Cliff in providing the royal entertainment. The power of the Establishment is manifest. One of its worst abuses was when Princess Margaret got married and the British military had sixpence deducted from the soldiers wages to buy her a present. The military hierarchy also all receive gongs when they reach a certain level of seniority.

Q: SO IT'S NOT JUST SUCCESS WHICH MERITS A GONG, IT HELPS TO BE PRO-ESTABLISHMENT?

A: Indeed. Sean Connery, the biggest British box-office attraction ever, had to wait until he could draw his pension before being recognised by the state, but then he is a Scottish Nationalist. In an exclusive interview with the *Herald* in March 2003 Connery revealed that New Labour had indeed blocked his knighthood because of his SNP involvement. The 'real' reason hinted at was that Connery had once allegedly condoned domestic violence but it is generally accepted that this was a mere political smokescreen.

Connery's mate Michael Caine had to wait decades to be recognised. *He wasn't a Scottish Nationalist as well?* No, he was a Cockney boy but he loathed British class divisiveness (as did Connery) and preferred to live in the USA. Also, he played many working-class roles and it helps if one plays posh, up-market roles as did Olivier, Gielgud, Redgrave, McKellen and the other prominent actors. There have been some surprises though — Mick Jagger did as much for British pop music as anyone, but he was on the wild side and once declined to play at a Royal Variety show as the cosy conformity and gushing sycophancy of the evening would spoil the spit-in-your-eye image of the Rolling Stones.

However, the insidious nature of gong-dangling seems to overpower all but the most fiercely independent. Jagger succumbed and accepted a knighthood in December 2003, much to the chagrin of his Stones' colleague Keith Richards who said, with some rather confused imagery, that being kitted out in 'a fucking coronet, draped in ermine' was not 'what the Stones were about'. Sir Mick countered that Keith was jealous. Adult, or what?

Q: SO WHAT CHANGED? WHO NOMINATED HIM?

A: Many eyebrows were raised, as Mick Jagger's moral fibre was not perhaps the stuff Sunday school teachers were made of, but you can bet your bottom dollar the gong was the idea of the immensely populist Tony Blair.

Populist? It is said, if Mr Blair were a stick of rock he would have 'Please Love Me' printed right the way through him.

Wouldn't Jagger have to accept it in the first place? There's the rub. Clearly Jagger wanted the gong or he would have declined the offer when it was put to him that he might be in line for one. Surprisingly, Mick's long-term friend Marianne Faithful revealed in a radio interview in July 2002 that underneath it all he was a 'most frightful snob'.

Q: WHAT ABOUT BILLY CONNOLLY? SURELY HE'S PUT MORE FANNIES ... SORRY, BUTTS, ON SEATS THAN MOST?

A: We tend to use the term 'bums on seats' in the UK (see Swearing on page 70), but you're right. Billy Connolly has played to packed houses all over the UK and the Commonwealth; he has also made some good movies (and some howlers). Had he attracted smaller audiences, but concentrated on Shakespeare and the classics, the gong would be assured. He had the temerity to focus his comedy on body parts, bodily functions and other vulgar subjects though, which is not really how PLU (people like us) behave. However, he has made friends in high places and for reasons best known to himself he has been scathing about the Scottish Parliament calling it 'a pretendy wee parliament', so who knows ... Mr Blair did award him, as a token gesture, a second-rate CBE. As the irreverent Billy was prepared to accept it, the door is now open for something bigger and better. Many lesser known Scots in show business have been honoured, such as Brian Cox,

Robert Carlyle (the psycho Begbie in **Trainspotting**), John Byrne, Tom Fleming and racing driver Jackie Stewart. It is possible Billy Connolly was offered a gong earlier but declined. A touch of sycophancy towards the Establishment can be helpful.

Q: BOB GELDOF WASN'T ALL THAT SYCOPHANTIC?

A: True, Bob was of the unkempt, long-haired and rebellious mould of Mick Jagger but, as an Irish citizen, he couldn't be called Sir so the feelings of all those time-serving generals, admirals and senior civil servants could be spared.

Really? You bet — the British Establishment pecking order is a force to be reckoned with. When the Beatles were awarded MBEs by that cunning old Prime Minister, Harold Wilson, several of the old-school recipients sent their medals back not wishing to be associated with common little pop singers with Scouse accents. Perhaps the worst example of class division was the existence of two similar medals, the MBE and the BEM, the former reserved exclusively for 'the officer class' and the latter for other ranks. When the first men to row the Atlantic in 1966, John Ridgway and Chay Blyth – both soldiers – accomplished this heroic feat, Ridgway (a commissioned officer) was awarded the MBE and Blyth (a working-class soldier) got the BEM. Fortunately, the incident helped to highlight such iniquities and the BEM was scrapped shortly after. Incidentally, Blyth then sailed single-handed round the world the wrong way in 1971 and promptly accepted a CBE for it!

Q: ARE THERE DIFFERENCES BETWEEN SCOTTISH AND ENGLISH ACCEPTANCE OF THESE AWARDS?

A: Obviously there will always be an English majority because of the population ratio. However, we can never know for certain who has refused these gongs. Downing Street is very crafty in that it writes to proposed recipients using the conditional tense suggesting that one's name may be 'put forward' for inclusion in the next honours list and should a decision be made in favour of granting an award, would the recipient be favourably disposed to accepting it? Should the proposed recipient write back angrily saying that these awards are elitist baubles which have no relevance in a modern democratic society, the palace will conveniently find that the recommendation did not reach the final rubber-stamp of approval. So it is almost impossible to quantify the refuseniks. It is generally understood that most writers have been rather disparaging about these awards and there is a noticeable absence of our great authors among the ranks of the honoured. The most famous refusal in recent history was Benjamin

Zephaniah, the black West Indian poet. With all the subtlety of a plane crash the Establishment offered this descendent of the slave trade, not a Companion of Honour or an Order of Merit – which at least sound inoffensive – but invited him to be an Officer of the Order of the British Empire. Just a casual glance through the writings of Benjamin would detect a strong theme of resentment at all white supremacist values. To offer the man an OBE shows a quite breathtaking level of insensitivity which finds its roots in the assumption that all recipients are vain sycophants who can't wait to be patronised by the royal hand. Tony Blair's populism can be seen at work here. No disrespect to Benjamin but the Rastafarian poet is relatively unknown compared with other gong recipients. Mr Blair's enthusiasm to bring the black brother 'on-side' blinded him to the insult potential of the offer.

Q: So THE ROYAL MEDAL DISTRIBUTION IS NOT ALL SWEETNESS AND LIGHT?

A: A document leaked to *The Times* in December 2003 by a civil servant listed some 300 refusniks who turned down such medals considering them to be unacceptable. The list included novelist JG Ballard, artist Lucien Freud, actor Albert Finney, jazz musician and broadcaster Humphrey Lyttelton and pop star David Bowie.

The power of patronage has tended to arouse suspicions of favouritism in many quarters. Many Scottish Catholics have expressed such suspicion regarding the award of the Order of the Thistle. As yet, after several centuries, no Catholic has ever been a recipient. Tom Devine, a Scottish Catholic academic, has dismissed such perceived victimisation as paranoia — but it is not difficult to understand how such feelings arise.

Q: WHAT WOULD THESE GONGS BE REPLACED BY?

A: The biblical exhortation to remove the beam from one's own eye before wishing to remove the mote from one's neighbour's has usually been lost on the British. The tendency to snigger at foreign countries for over-elaborate pomp, for example. We giggled when Uganda's Idi Amin elevated himself to the rank of Field Marshal yet we promoted the Queen's husband from lowly Lieutenant to Admiral of the Fleet in one fell swoop, at the same time making him a Prince, a Duke and a Baron not to mention awarding him all sorts of hardware to wear on his manly bosom.

There used to be British condescension towards the USSR's gongs, such as the Red Star 3rd Class or 4th Class, while we dished out 22 classes of awards. Italy's highest civil award is the very sensible and logical Gold Medal. The American gong, the Congressional Medal of Honour, has a sensible ring to it as do the French Legion d'honeur and our own Order of Merit — but all these ludicrous allusions to the Empire, Garters and Bedchambers really have to go. One theory was that we should adopt the academic grading system.

Q: YOU MEAN AS IN A, B, C, ETC?

A: Precisely, so at each honours distribution, instead of old boys in their clubs muttering, 'I see old Carruthers got his Garter,' we might hear, 'Old Simpkins was given a D and I'll be damned if old Crabtree didn't get a C.' Work of a superlatively high order over and above the call of duty might merit an A and long-serving foot soldiers who have worked dutifully for the community might be awarded a D or an E. Status-seeking snobs might be appalled at such utilitarian changes but it really is only a matter of time. Even our high-church clerics – the followers of Christ, whose entire message was one of simplicity and humility – will quote from the pulpit that he who exalteth himself shall be humbled, yet they adopt titles such as Reverend, Very Reverend, Right Reverend and Your Grace and apply a hierarchical structure wholly anathema to the Christian message. The low churches, the Church of Scotland, Methodists, Baptists etc eschew such rankings. Most nations get by without any award system at all.

Q: I'M GLAD WE DON'T HAVE ALL THIS NONSENSE IN THE STATES

A: Maybe, but you are not impervious to it. Your Alan Greenspan, Chairman of the Federal Reserve Board, accepted a knighthood for his contribution to 'economic stability'. As a Yank he was told he couldn't call himself 'Sir' but he could put KBE after his name, though it is difficult to see which is the sillier; a Sir in front or a suffix of Grand Knight Commander of the Order of the British Empire. One wonders just how long it took the Romans to stop alluding to their empire.

Q: BUT BACK TO INDEPENDENCE: SURELY THERE ARE SCOTTISH ARISTOS IN FAVOUR?

A: It is unlikely, as it is really against their very nature. Back in 1707 the people had no vote so it was a tiny coterie of Scottish noblemen (not to be confused with noble men) who sold Scotland's independence 'for English gold', to quote Robert Burns, who described them as 'a parcel of rogues in a nation'. The people of Scotland were fiercely hostile to the Act of Union but the magnates had just about bankrupted Scotland with the disastrous Darien Scheme seven years earlier. The temptation to regain their money for a mere loss of national independence was too great. So this undemocratic and mercenary Faustian bargain was struck. Scottish aristocrats have always had more in common with their English counterparts than with their own people.

Q: WHAT WAS THE DARIEN SCHEME?

A: By the end of the 17th century England, Spain and Holland had achieved highly profitable colonial successes and established trade routes to the east and the west. Scotland, keen for a piece of the action, established The Company of Scotland Trading to Africa and The Indies. The keystone to their trading plans was the establishment of a colony on the isthmus of Darien, now Panama. William Paterson was the driving force behind the scheme and he managed to attract backing amounting to £400,000 — a vast sum in 1698. Paterson set up the colony of New Edinburgh but fever, dissension and English opposition, not to mention the four months sailing time, ruined the venture. Despite many deaths – of the 1200 who sailed to Darien, 400 died – disease, lack of food and a plague of mosquitoes, a second expedition set sail in 1699 with 1300 people. This time fire destroyed the ship carrying all their food. They clung on till March 1700 when they were forced to sign Articles of Capitulation for the Spanish. Only a handful survived the return journey. The colony was abandoned with the loss of over 2000 people and roughly £200,000 of capital.

Q: WHY DO YOU SAY SCOTTISH ARISTOCRATS HAD MORE IN COMMON WITH THEIR ENGLISH COUNTERPARTS THAN THEIR OWN PEOPLE?

A: It began in March 1603 when James VI of Scotland inherited the English throne on the death of Elizabeth I, the virgin Queen of England. He became James I of Great Britain. Had he chosen to maintain his court in Scotland things might have been different, but he chose London. So the fount of all power, titles, favours and patronage came from London. Within a generation the guid Scots tongue could no longer be heard in the royal corridors. The Scottish aristocrats slowly lost their native tongue too and began to ape the southern vowel sounds (and missing consonants) of the court. Their offspring were sent either to private schools in Scotland where English speech was favoured or to the prestigious ones in England such as Eton, Harrow or Winchester. To this day, all the Scottish Dukes, Earls etc sound indistinguishable from their English equivalents. The contrast is most striking in places like the Borders where the rich accents of Galashiels, Selkirk or Melrose can be heard alongside the cultivated sounds of Mayfair as the local laird shops for some boxes of 12-bore cartridges.

Q: AREN'T SCOTTISH NOBLES PATRIOTIC SCOTS?

A: Perhaps when Scotland had its own monarchy but, after 1603, the title-hungry could only look southwards. Titles, gongs and patronage come from the monarchical structure — you cannot be a Knight or Peer of the realm if there is no realm. You cannot hire the antiquated garb known as 'morning dress' complete with top hat and then queue at the palace to receive your MBE if there is no palace. So all the great and the good simply must support the monarchy and by extension the Union. Even with devolution (a sort of semi-independence) the so-called 'NO-NO' campaigners in the referendum of 1997 (two NO's — one against devolution and one against tax-raising powers) consisted of most of the prominent titled people in Scotland.

In some respects the titled Scots are just a tad schizophrenic. They may take pride in their long Scottish heritage, wear the kilt on ceremonial occasions and even recite some Burns, though perhaps avoiding the bits about their rank being just the guinea stamp.

Guinea stamp?

Burns' poetry has a theme of egalitarianism and iconoclasm running through it. His line that rank is but the 'guinea stamp' alludes to an old sum of money, the guinea (one pound and one shilling), which made the possession of rank or property official. Burns dismisses all this with, 'a man's a man for a' that'.

So, though the Scottish aristocracy may express pride in their Scottishness, ask them to acquire a Scots accent or stop sending their offspring to expensive private English schools and they will look mystified.

Some of this split-personality thinking has rubbed off on the Scottish people. One can hear people use the term 'well-spoken' when alluding to someone with a refined English accent. In Ireland, where the link with the monarchy and the Westminster parliament is just a folk-memory, people seeking the same description would say, 'the man with the English accent'.

Q: SURELY ALL THE RECIPIENTS OF TITLES DON'T THINK ALIKE?

A: Some argue that as titles and gongs are given for such a diverse range of achievements, there is no great risk of homogeneity of thought or action amongst the recipients. Maybe, but they are all pretty well guaranteed to be pro-monarchist and pro-Establishment. The diversity angle has some merit but take for example Scottish devolution. This has been agitated for in Scotland since the time of Keir Hardy. It was denied the Scots under a rigged referendum in 1979 when a codicil was put in the plebiscite that 40% of the people had to vote for it. With many constituencies not even reaching a 40% turn out, the likelihood of 40% voting 'for' was destined to fail. Though devolution achieved a majority it, predictably, did not reach the threshold so Scots were denied a devolved system of government. When the next devolution referendum came round in 1997 the 'Yes' campaign was led by Donald Dewar, Alex Salmond and Jim Wallace in a Lab/SNP/LibDem alliance.

The 'No' campaign was supported by the titled and gonged, to wit, Sir Michael Forsyth, Sir Matthew Goodwin, Sir Michael Hurst, Sir Malcolm Rifkind, Sir Bruce Pattullo, Sir Adrian Shinwell (yes, his forebear Manny, the firebrand Socialist would have turned in his grave), Lord Mackay, Lord Laing, Lord Strathclyde and a few other lesser OBEs, MBEs etc. Every one a Tory, and all recipients of the magic alphabet soup. Not forgetting (Lord) Michael Ancrum and (Lord) James Douglas Hamilton, both heirs to more titles than MGM. The only conspicuous Labour supporter of the 'No' campaign was Tam Dalyell although Tam had been educated at the English epi-centre of Establishment values, Eton College.

Q: WHICH COMES FIRST, THE TITLES OR THE LEANINGS?

A: Hard to say for sure. Real left-wingers or democratic republicans would not accept the gongs in the first place. Fence sitters are probably brought 'on-side' by the gongs. It would be very difficult to express anti-Establishment opinions having received an OBE or a knighthood. Clement Attlee, the PM who gave us the Socialist concept of a welfare state, accepted a peerage. Two generations later his grandson, Lord Attlee, crossed the floor of the House of Lords and joined the Conservative benches.

Q: WASN'T THAT A BETRAYAL OF HIS GRANDPA?

A: Very much so. But titles have that effect.

Q: ISN'T THERE A SAYING 'EVERYONE LOVES A LORD'?

A: The sentiment may exist in England but Scotland has a more egalitarian view of these things. **Why?** Church of Scotland Presbyterianism (or The Kirk) is a highly democratic institution. It has no hierarchy as do the Anglo and Roman Catholic churches with archbishops, bishops, canons etc. The kirk minister is chosen by the congregation and if he cannot cut the mustard he is fired. This has influenced Scottish thinking since the Reformation. So, deference and forelock-tugging to the nobility is not as widespread as down south. Also, some of the greatest crimes against the Scottish people have been committed by Scottish nobles.

Such as? Well, in the 12th century they accepted Edward I as Lord Superior, then their sale of Scotland's independence in 1707 against the wishes of the Scottish people. Perhaps the most heinous act of human cruelty perpetrated by the nobles against their own people was the Highland clearances of the 19th century when subsistence farmers were swept from the land to make way for more profitable Cheviot sheep. These callous and greedy acts could be epitomised by the clearance of the estate belonging to the Countess of Sutherland and Lord Stafford who owned two-thirds of Sutherland in the northern Highlands. From 1807 to 1821 their factors executed the plans of their agent James Loch to clear the estate.

The Duke of Atholl was responsible for clearing Glen Tilt, but all the Highland landlords were complicit in these dreadful deeds. Worse, many of them were absentee landlords who maintained lavish lifestyles in London rubbing shoulders with the other landlords who owned great swathes of Scotland, England and Ireland. They left the dirty work to their agents, one of whom, Patrick Sellar, was so diligently brutal in his clearance of Strathnaver in 1814 that he was tried for his cruelty. In areas the systematic brutality was so great that some glens are still empty, as in Glengarry where the McDonnells were the landowners.

Q: WERE PEOPLE CLEARED ONLY FROM THE HIGHLANDS?

A: No. The agricultural revolution which began in the 18th century and continued into the 19th caused the displacement of many rural families in the Lowlands. Those Lowlanders who were not absorbed by the factories of the new industrial revolution were forced to migrate in their thousands.

Q: WHERE DID THE PEOPLE GO?

A: For balance it should be stated that life in the Highlands was never idyllic. Life was very hard and hunger was never far from the door. Also, a pattern of emigration had been established from the time of the Reformation and Presbyterian conflict with the established church. The concept of a better life elsewhere had some appeal which helped ameliorate the appalling wrench of leaving one's homeland. Additionally, the dreadful potato famine, which blighted Ireland in 1845, hit Scotland in 1846. The great Scottish diaspora that began with the Plantation of Ulster in the 17th century peaked at the time of the clearances and the potato blight. People migrated to Canada, America, Australia, New Zealand and South Africa. Many of the placenames in the English speaking New World reflect Scottish roots, such as Nova Scotia, Perth, Dunedin, Dallas and McKenzie Country. Two of the more famous defenders of the Alamo in Texas, Jim Bowie and Davy Crockett, were of Scottish blood. Crockett's hardware store in Glasgow's West Nile St was established by Davy's kith and kin.

Q: HOW DID THESE SCOTTISH ARISTOS ACQUIRE THEIR LANDS AND TITLES IN THE FIRST PLACE?

A: Almost every citation awarding these titles will contain the words 'for services to the King'. Not one reads 'for services to the people'. These services could be almost any act that gratified the monarch. In some cases it might have been an act of bravery such as fighting alongside the king in battle or it could be a reward for turning a blind eye to the king's sexual dalliance with one's wife and should the illicit union produce a child, that child could be the recipient of yet another title. Lands and titles were quite simply bestowed to favourites. There were only two dukedoms awarded for merit — Marlborough and Wellington. All the rest were just gifts to favourites or family.

Such as?

Take Charles II. He had four children from four different women — Nell Gwynn, the Duchesses of Cleveland and Portsmouth, and Lucy Walters. The royal bastards became respectively the Dukes of St Albans, Grafton, Richmond and Buccleuch. Ironically, dukes are top of the hierarchical pecking order yet have by far the most ignoble origins.

The least corrupt distribution of titles was during the prime ministerial term of Lloyd George (1863-1945) who openly sold the titles that the rich yearned for, a precedent set by James VI who used titles to fill the royal coffers. As Hesketh Pearson put it in **The Pilgrim Daughters** — 'There is no stronger craving in the world than that of the rich for titles, except perhaps that of the titled for riches'. Lloyd George put a price tag of £50,000 on a peerage and £10,000 on a knighthood. In today's money, these were truly vast sums to pay, but there was no shortage of takers. A sardonic comment of the period on the purchase of honours was made by the (soon to be) Lord Northcliffe who said, 'When I want a peerage, I shall buy it like an honest man'. Despite his radicalism, Lloyd George accepted an earldom.

In Scotland, rank has always been viewed with disdain and in keeping with Burns' sentiment of being just the 'guinea stamp'.

Q: SO THE SCOTS ARE NOT TOO KEEN ON THEIR NOBLES?

A: Not very, neither are the Welsh. Lloyd George himself had his early politics moulded by the hatred a Welsh-speaking nonconformist peasantry felt for its English and Anglican landlords. He entered politics as a radical Welsh nationalist. The Irish are probably the most laid back about such issues; despite Ireland being an independent republic, there are still titles floating about such as the Countess of Athlone or Lord Longford, but no-one seems to mind.

Q: BUT DIDN'T THE IRISH BLOW UP NELSON'S COLUMN IN DUBLIN?

A: Well yes, actually it was called Nelson's Pillar lest it be confused with the one in London's Trafalgar Square. After Home Rule in 1922, Ireland was still awash with placenames and street names bestowed by the colonial British. Many of the more prominent place names were changed so Sackville St became O'Connell St. However, the Irish knew they could not airbrush away unpleasant associations of their colonial past, so most of the old British placenames remain — Landsdowne Rd, Grafton St, Waterloo, Wellington, Raglan, George and many more. Some were too much to bear: Queen Victoria's statue outside the Dail had to go, as did King Billy's statue in nearby St Stephen's Green.

The most obvious was the presence of Nelson's Pillar dominating O'Connell St and situated just outside the epi-centre and icon of the Easter Rising, the General Post Office. A necklace of plastic explosive was draped around the pillar by a (forgive the pun) splinter group of the IRA and the bold admiral was dispatched, with some velocity, into an adjacent, and fortunately empty, taxi rank. Rumour has it that the IRA was invited by persons unknown in Scotland to carry out the same operation on the plinth of the Duke of Sutherland's monument at Golspie that acts as a constant reminder of the cruelty of the Highland clearances to those in the area.

Q: WHAT PRECISELY IS THE HOUSE OF LORDS AND A HOUSE OF COMMONS?

A: Most democracies have a bi-cameral parliament. One house, the lower house, will normally debate and vote on the laws of the land and then pass the bills to the upper house for scrutiny. Our upper house is still known as the House of Lords.

Q: HOW DOES THE HOUSE OF LORDS COMPARE WITH, SAY, THE US SENATE?

A: In a word, it doesn't. The only similarity is their function. Both represent the upper house and as such are a revising chamber for legislation passed in the House of Commons or the House of Representatives. As to their composition, there any similarity ends. It is hard to believe but until the Blair reforms of the Lords, there were almost 1200 peers entitled to sit in the House of Lords. *Twelve hundred! You've got to be kidding!* No — and it gets worse. In the US Senate there are 100 senators, two for each state in the union. Britain, which could fit easily into Texas, had — to be precise — 1195 peers.

You say it gets worse? Much worse. Of the 1200, two-thirds were there purely through an accident of birth — they were the eldest sons of a peer. *No daughters?* No, it always was, and remains to a lesser extent, sexist. Under the rule of male primogeniture ... *What?* ... First-born, but not just first-born – first-male-born, so half a dozen older sisters wouldn't count – the male got the title and the seat in the Lords. *No other qualification?* None. He could be dishonourable, dyslexic, dysfunctional, dishonest or dissipated – it made no difference. In fact, had honour, integrity and intelligence been prerequisites, the house would never have survived.

Q: WEREN'T THE HEREDITARIES RATHER A HARMLESS LOT?

A: There were some fine minds and some very good debates and often the Lords as a revising chamber would send back bills to the Commons which were badly drafted or ill-considered, but apart from the iniquity of a hereditary seat, there were other aspects of bias. *Such as?* For a start, being peers of the realm, they would be pro-Establishment thus loading the chamber with a Conservative bias. Also, being a homogenous breed, they would be bound to vote for their own sectional interests. *Like what?* One example might be fox-hunting which the landed gentry would be unlikely to vote against. Another crass example was when Margaret Thatcher wished to remove the rates system and introduce the poll tax. *Explain?* The rates system was where local taxation was based upon the value of your house and estates. The poll tax was levied on every occupant aged 18 or over in any household. So if a duke lived in a castle with vast estates, he paid very high rates directly proportionate to the value of his home and lands. A poor family in a small terraced house would pay a great deal less.

The poll tax meant that the wealthy duke and duchess paid exactly the same per head as an impoverished Mr and Mrs McNumptie. When the Poll Tax Bill reached the Lords, it was packed. Hereditary peers who had never before darkened the place's door thronged into the upper house to vote enthusiastically for it. A basic rule of jurisprudence is that no-one should arbitrate in a matter in which one has a vested interest. The Lords' massive majority for the poll tax was quite simply a scandal.

Q: SO YOUR UPPER HOUSE HAD A POLITICAL BIAS AS WELL AS BEING SEXIST AND RACIST?

A: Worse than racist; racism is the discrimination of the grounds of ethnic origin, this system was nepotic, it kept the seat exclusively for the same family. *Isn't that illegal?* Technically yes. But there's more. The Lords also discriminates on religious grounds. The monarch is the Head of the Church of England, her English bishops – all 26 of them – are automatically entitled to a seat in the upper house. *What about the Catholic Bishops?* No, not entitled. Nor are the heads of Sikh, Buddhist, Muslim, Hindu or Jewish faiths — nor the other Protestant faiths such as the Presbyterians, Baptists, Methodists etc. *Don't you have laws against these things?* Possibly the greatest irony of all is that the House of Lords is the highest law court in the land. The Law Lords – all 12 of them – have a seat in this den of, quite literally, iniquity.

Q: YOU BRITS AMAZE ME. SO WHAT WERE THE BLAIR REFORMS?

A: To put it into perspective the house has been reformed several times. For centuries there were no women at all in the Lords and in 1958 'life peerages' were introduced so the nepotism could be watered down. Blair slashed the number of hereditary seats from just over 600 to 92 and the 92 were chosen by the house itself.

Q: WHY 92 HEREDITARY PEERS — THAT'S STILL ALMOST AS MANY AS THE US SENATE?

A: Why any? — is the real question. Why should anyone expect a seat in the upper house simply as a birthright? But their days are numbered.

Q: SO SOON THEY'LL ALL BE LIFE PEERS? YOU MEAN A JOB FOR LIFE?

A: Yes, it is still hopelessly undemocratic. The people have no say whatsoever. Also, although Tony Blair swept away almost all of the hereditary peers, approximately 600 peers still remain, including the Anglican bishops, the Law Lords and the 92 hereditary peers. To put it into perspective that is six times as many as the most powerful nation on the planet, the USA.

Q: SO WHO APPOINTS THE LIFE PEERS?

A: In effect, the government of the day. It could stack the house with its own placemen ... and it does. Tony Blair has actually created more life peers than did Margaret Thatcher. One thing he did introduce was 'people's peers'. *Ordinary working-class men and women?* It sounds it but alas, the people's peers were all selected from the great and good and they blended seamlessly with the existing incumbents. The government does try to apply a degree of proportionality in that the other political parties will have nominees for the Lords and they will generally be accepted, but the bias remains in the government's favour.

Q: SOUNDS LIKE YOU NEED TO SCRAP THE WHOLE THING AND START AGAIN?

A: In any mature democracy, that is precisely what would happen. The very name House of Lords should be consigned to the dustbin of history along with the memory of racism, nepotism, elitism, sexism, religious discrimination and unearned deference. **Unearned deference?** Yes, even in the third millennium AD many of the great British public are still fitted with grovel buttons and are genetically programmed to genuflect at the sound of an approaching Peer of the Realm. Most peculiar of all, the hereditary peers – whose only achievement is in being born – seem to attract more subservience than the life peers.

Q: WHAT'S GOING TO HAPPEN TO THE UPPER HOUSE?

A: Very hard to say. In a parliamentary ballot in February 2003, six different options were placed before the House of Commons, ranging from an all-elected upper house to an all-appointed house. No one option was given clear support. So the question of the composition of the upper house remains unsolved.

Q: OK. BUT YOUR HOUSE OF COMMONS IS DEMOCRAT-ICALLY ELECTED?

A: Yes it is. But, although elected by the people, it too is numerically top-heavy. The UK population is just under 60 million and we have just over 650 MPs. In round figures that is one for every 90,000 people. California alone has 31 million people with just 52 congressmen (and only two senators), that is one congressman for every 600,000 people. **Yes, but the US has the legislature of the individual states.** True, but Scotland for example, with fewer people than the state of Indiana, has 129 MSPs on top of the 72 it sends to Westminster plus there are the 32 Regional Councils which administer the needs of the local community.

Q: WOULD AN INDEPENDENT SCOTLAND RETAIN THE MONARCHY?

A: Common sense would dictate that if Scotland is going to become an independent nation with its own small defence force, its own full parliament, its own taxation system, its own flag ... it really needs a completely clean break and that means a democratically elected head of state and a severance from the monarchy. Most of the Commonwealth countries did so. Ireland not only jettisoned the British yoke but chose to leave the Commonwealth as well — and as a small independent country within the European Union it seems to be doing quite nicely. It broke the link with the UK currency, Sterling, and as of January 2002 started trading in Euros.

Australia would have voted to ditch the monarchy at their referendum only the alternative method of electing a head of state was not to their liking, so the monarchy remained purely by default. The next Aussie referendum on the issue will see the end of a hereditary head of state who lives 12,000 miles away. Already they have scrapped God Save the Queen as their national anthem and the reference to the monarch in the national citizen's oath of allegiance. They abandoned the acceptance of alphabet soup some years ago, so knighthoods, MBEs etc remain a peculiarly British idiosyncrasy. New Zealand also retains the British monarch as head of state but the current Prime Minister, Helen Clark, makes no secret of her republican stance.

Q: WHAT ABOUT THE NOSTALGIA FACTOR?

A: Not to be dismissed. A sizeable number of Aussies and Kiwis are first-generation Brits who still have a sentimental attachment to the old country and retain a certain regard for the monarchy they left behind. However the younger folk and more importantly those with mainland European or Asian roots do not have the same affiliations. Emotions aside, logic will prevail. In 2003, the Governor General of Australia, Peter Hollingworth, the Queen's envoy in Australia, was forced to resign. As an erstwhile bishop he had protected a paedophile priest while he himself had been accused of rape (a claim later retracted by the family of the alleged victim who then committed suicide). Strong stuff for an elected representative of the people but, for an unelected representative of the British monarch appointed by the pro-monarchy Prime Minister, John Howard, this will only inflame pro-republican passions.

Q: WHY DON'T THE SCOTS NATIONALISTS ANNOUNCE REPUBLICANISM AS POLICY?

A: The party is a little disingenuous on this issue. Most SNP members want rid of the monarchy but, because there is a sentimental attachment to it throughout Scotland, especially among the senior citizens, there are votes to be lost in appearing too hostile to the institution. They choose instead the soft option and say that a referendum would have to be held on the question. Far more honest to say that the SNP sees the monarchy as an outdated, undemocratic bastion of old-fashioned class division and has no part in a modern Scotland. Blisteringly honest but alas not the way of politicians.

45

Q: WE THOUGHT EVERYBODY LOVED THE MONARCHY?

A: Certainly that is the impression given by much of our media. With many of the media barons being recipients of monarchical gongs they are unlikely to campaign for a republic.

The feelings of the people in general fluctuate. The golden era was when a lovely young queen married her handsome sailor and produced some nice looking children. The 60s saw a much less subservient generation assert itself through rock 'n' roll, flower power, free love, student riots, anti-Vietnam war protests, ban the bomb marches and an entire youth culture. Since then, although the monarch herself has seldom put a foot wrong, the other royals have brought the institution into disrepute. While the palace works hard on pro-monarchy public relations, there are some unpleasant odours which cannot be disguised. Philip's notoriety for his tactless and often racist remarks hasn't helped.

Q: WHAT ABOUT THE LATE QUEEN MOTHER?

A: It is hard to tell where genuine affection ends and Establishment hype begins. In the deluge of obsequiousness which surrounded her passing, the media managed to credit her with just four achievements. Firstly, she was a 'lovely' person. Most grandmothers are, and if acting graciously is all that one is required to do, it doesn't seem too onerous a task. Secondly she reached the venerable age of 101. That is indeed an achievement but one has to wonder just how many of Scotland's premature dead would have reached such advanced years had they been freed from worry, work, poverty, stress, bad nutrition and hospital waiting lists. Thirdly, she heroically insisted that she and her vapid husband remain in London throughout the blitz. What was the alternative? What sort of example would the head of state have set by fleeing the country to Canada in time of war. Also, anyone familiar with the tunnel system under Buckingham Palace leading to Whitehall will confirm the royals were as safe as Fort Knox.

The statement which is most quoted about the Queen Mum was her rather insulting comment that she could look the East End in the eye after some of the Buck House brickwork was damaged by the Luftwaffe. The East End along with Coventry and Clydebank, just to the west of Glasgow, were absolutely pulverised and any East Ender being looked 'in the eye' by a fabulously wealthy, multi-homed aristocrat might not have shared the then Queen's peculiar view of equality. A Channel 4 TV programme, Secret History, revealed that there was widespread resentment amongst London's East Enders when royals went walkabout in their rubble.

Q: THE US PRESS GIVES YOUR ROYALS WIDE COVERAGE.

A: The Brits are aware of this and many of the pro-monarchists argue that Americans are envious of the British monarchical system. When Americans are asked about this they generally concede that many US citizens are fascinated by the concept of monarchy and all the pomp and circumstance which surrounds it, but envy is not very much in evidence.

Q: SO THE ROYALS' POPULARITY RISES AND FALLS?

A: Very much so. The Georges were very unpopular. George I couldn't speak English. George II could but preferred to speak German. George III, apart from going mad, managed to alienate the Americans and lose the colony while George IV was an obese and useless playboy. Victoria was in the doghouse for a number of years when she withdrew from public life after the death of her husband, Albert. As her years and the Empire advanced she regained popularity and she became a figure of reverence. The current royals' popularity was plummeting until Diana came along. She proved to be the best of times and the worst of times. This glamorous, warm-hearted girl was the best PR the palace had seen for decades. She had bearing, charm, graciousness and height — a feature singularly lacking in many of our royals.

The dysfunctional royals bathed in Diana's reflected glory while at the same time treating her abominably. Warmth and demonstrative affection were never strong suits in the family but they even lowered the temperature towards Diana. Slowly the nation became aware of Diana's unhappiness with her in-laws and when the news broke that Charles had continued his affair with the rather matronly Camilla, the royals reached a new low with the public. Diana's death sent shockwaves throughout the land and the world in general. The normally obsequious press had to challenge the royals to fly the palace flag at half-mast. The palace muttered that it was contrary to royal protocol. Who cares, cried the people, lower the bloody flag. The palace relented and the flag was lowered. Had a referendum been taken after the accusatory speech of Diana's brother at her funeral, the monarchy would have received a vote of no confidence.

Q: WHAT KEEPS THE MONARCHY IN PLACE?

A: The best PR is probably the Queen herself. If somebody has to do the job of being the reigning monarch, she does it as well as anyone could ask. Long service is also a great asset. Fifty years on the throne may have, albeit temporarily, imbued the people with renewed loyalty and affection.

Q: SPAIN MANAGED TO RE-INTRODUCE THE MONARCHY AND IT SEEMS QUITE POPULAR.

A: Yes, but it was what went before which made the restoration acceptable. For almost 40 years Franco had been an absolute monarch in all but name. The introduction of a moderate and democratic monarchical system was quite appealing by comparison. Also Juan Carlos has carefully cultivated the image of a hard-working head of state. His image on TV at close-down time shows him at work behind his desk. The Scandinavian and Dutch monarchies all encourage that common touch without too much ceremony. These families manage to move about their realms (often on bicycles) without bringing the country to a standstill. The hostility to the British monarchy stemmed not so much from having a hereditary head of state as opposed to a president but instead came from the endless level of hangers-on and beneficiaries who, with the vast expense necessary to maintain the entire system, don't seem to do very much.

Q: YOUR COUNTRY WOULD BE A LOT LESS COLOURFUL WOULDN'T IT?

A: Fair point. Many anti-monarchists would probably settle for an unelected head of state if some of the more offensive Ruritanian trimmings could be scrapped. Take the opening of parliament after the long summer recess. Historically, the Queen sits in the palace of the unelected House of Lords in a ballgown a drag queen would die for. There the entire gathering is awash with ermine, sable, crowns, coronets, medals, badges, sparkling gowns, tights with garters and flunkeys in wigs. When their Lordships are ready, they send Black Rod to chap the door of the democratically elected House of Commons. The MPs then respectfully file in dressed in their drab business suits and are forced to stand while the monarch reads a speech that the Prime Minister has written.

Q: HOW DID THE QUEEN'S JUBILEE AFFECT PUBLIC OPINION?

A: Without a doubt there was a wave of goodwill towards the Queen on her '50th' helped of course by the pro-royalist media. The cameras homed in on the devoted royalists at the railings of

Buckingham Palace intoning, 'Gawd bless her, isn't she marvellous'. How the remainder of the population reacted is difficult to ascertain. There will be many who occupy Britain's great inner city squalor or the peripheral housing schemes whose views are not canvassed.

Q: STILL, 50 YEARS IS NOT TO BE SNEEZED AT.

A: True, anyone who achieves a 'fiftieth' deserves appreciation and recognition. Even the staunchest republicans were reluctant to pour cold water on the occasion particularly with regard to a woman who had lost both her sister and her mother in the same half year. Many observers believe that now the graph has peaked, it is only a matter of time before the line resumes its inexorable decline.

Q: AREN'T THE ROYALS GOOD FOR TOURISM?

A: Probably, but many visitors come to Britain for the country's history. Some argue that the history would exist with or without a reigning monarch. They claim that more people visit Versailles near Paris because it is open to the public whereas Buckingham Palace only allows very limited access. With English-speaking visitors from the US, Canada, Australia and New Zealand their motivation is mainly to trace family roots, an objective which is the backbone of the flourishing Irish Republic's tourist industry. A crucial factor in tourism is value for money and many visitors are shocked by British prices, especially those of London hotels. If prices are high, service should be good but we tend to fail in that area.

Q: ARE THERE ANY HARD STATISTICS OF APPROVAL OR OTHERWISE?

A: Not really. There have been polls on various royal questions. As we've seen popularity fluctuates. In the 1950s the UK-wide vote for the monarchy would have been in the 90% bracket (though a lower figure would be found in Scotland). One or two polls at the time of Diana's death showed a remarkable figure of a roughly 50/50 split. Now with the passage of time, even the Charles/Camilla relationship has gained general public approval. Young William seems to be a decent and pleasant young man; Philip no longer counts as he is considered generally gaga; Margaret and the Queen Mum are history and the lesser royals are no longer subject to media focus, so the popularity factor will slowly climb once again.

Q: MAYBE DEEP DOWN THE BRITS JUST LIKE THE CONCEPT OF MONARCHY?

A: Possibly. As children we all grew up with benevolent kings, fairy queens, beautiful princesses, brave and handsome princes, so somewhere in the psyche there may well be a nostalgic longing for a touch of magic. The relentless probing of the media's cameras coupled with too many examples of royal bad behaviour has let the genie out of the bottle. The news that Prince Charles (and others) regularly gave away gifts they had received from loyal subjects and visiting dignitaries, did not go down too well with the British public (nor with the donors). It may be coincidence but a poll in the *Sunday Mirror* of 16 March 2003 found that a majority of people considered Charles unfit to succeed as king and that the throne should pass to his son. In the same poll 21% expressed a preference for a republic.

Q: WHAT DO THE BRITS HAVE AGAINST THE EURO?

A: There has always been a strong conservative streak in the British. Some of it dates from the war years when Britain stood alone with the Wermacht parked on its very doorstep in the Channel Islands. All of mainland Europe had fallen to the Nazis. Events such as Dunkirk, the Battle of Britain and the blitz over London, Coventry and Clydebank helped cement a strong sense of independence in this island race. Added to this is the memory of a British Empire on which the sun never set.

Q: BUT SURELY THE EMPIRE MENTALITY IS HISTORY NOW?

A: Intellectually the British know that when the sun sets off Cornwall, that's it, apart from a sprinkling of rocks such as Gibraltar and the Falklands and, of course, that perennial thorn in Britain's side, Northern Ireland. Intellectually the people know Britannia no longer rules the waves; they see burgeoning European economies providing better health services, better pensions, infinitely better railways and roads, more holidays and shorter working weeks. However, the emotional has not quite caught up with the rational.

Deep down there is the conviction held by many that lesser mortals begin at Calais, that the World Cup rightfully belongs here; that India, Pakistan and the West Indies have all the luck when it comes to cricket, that British sportsmen and women play a cleaner, fairer game than those nasty foreigners. The very word foreign is an innocuous adjective yet has a pejorative ring to it in this green and pleasant land. Some British 'red topped' tabloid newspapers seem to relish castigating our neighbours.

John Major, the last Tory Prime Minister, expressed his rather misty-eyed patriotism when he spoke of long shadows on county cricket grounds, warm beer, invincible green suburbs, dog lovers and quoted George Orwell's line about old maids bicycling to Holy Communion in the morning mist. Unconsciously we do it all the time. Our Christmas cards are a kaleidoscope of horse-drawn coaches, woodsmen drawing sleds laden with Yule logs, scarlet-coated huntsmen riding through the snow or pheasants in flight over wintry rural settings.

Q: AHEM. THE EURO?

A: Sorry. Wandering a bit there, but the imagery is that of a people averse to change. Our joining of the original European Economic Community (aka the Common Market) seemed to go on forever. The right-wing press was continually banging on about our kith and kin in Australia, New Zealand and the other Commonwealth countries and how we were better aligning ourselves with these, mainly WASP people, rather than the Frogs, Krauts and Spicks across the Channel.

Why the EEC members wanted us to join them remains a mystery, although De Gaulle did manage to veto our joining in 1962 and again in 1969. Team-oriented we most certainly were not. However, we did join under Ted Heath's government in 1973. Weary MEPs from mainland Europe have grown to expect some British disagreement at the introduction of almost every piece of European legislation.

Q: BUT WOULDN'T EACH PIECE OF EU LEGISLATION BE JUDGED ON ITS INDIVIDUAL MERITS?

A: Ideally yes — but whether it is conservatism or sheer bloody-mindedness, Brits do not make good Europeans. We continue to drive on the wrong side of the road; though we now sell our milk in litres we insist our beer comes in pints; our Ordnance Survey maps show hills and distances in metres, yet our road signs stick doggedly to miles, our schoolchildren learn the metric system while the adults work in miles, yards, feet or even furlongs; we delight in reading about a rebellious greengrocer who insists on selling his produce in pounds and ounces. More serious non-compliance by the Brits involved various aspects of employment law, making it easier to dismiss employees in the UK than in most other European countries.

Our battle with the Euro fills many with a sense of déjà vu — we've been here before. When decimal currency was introduced in the early 70s, the same voices were raised in protest. Why anyone should wish to retain a currency which had eight half-crowns and two-hundred-and-forty pennies to the pound is a mystery.

The current conservative (and Conservative) cry is 'don't abolish the pound'. The erstwhile Tory leader Ian Duncan Smith went so far as to say that the Tories would never join the Euro. Yet the Bank of England abolished the pound note years ago (though the Scots retain it), the ten shilling note went, as did the half crown, the florin, the shilling, the sixpence the threepence, the penny, the halfpenny and the farthing. For that matter, we have abolished the groat, the sovereign, the guinea, the crown and the bawbee. We've done it all before. There is no great step for man nor mankind into the dark abyss of the unknown. To travel from the Turkish border to Portugal with no passport and with the same currency seems eminently sensible to all those peculiar foreigners across the English Channel and en passant across the Irish Sea. US citizens travel from Boston to Hawaii and from Alaska to Florida, through half a dozen time zones, using the same dollar. But the anti-Euro factions don't want any of that 'funny money'.

Q : ARE THE SCOTS FOR OR AGAINST THE EURO?

A : Generally for. Scotland is very much dependent on tourism for its income and many of the tourist centres will now accept the Euro. Currency is a UK issue, so there are few hard facts about Scottish preferences. Historically, Scotland has always had a more European outlook than England. How much this stemmed from a love of all things Continental or a hostility to their next door neighbour is difficult to quantify. The more prominent links with mainland Europe are the Auld Alliance formed with France in 1296 against the common enemy, Edward I of England; then Mary Queen of Scots who became Queen of France and a long history of trade with the Baltic states, the low countries and France.

The Firth of Forth was rich in fish and underneath the firth there was (and is) coal. Seawater was boiled in great pans on the firth to produce salt, hence placenames such as Prestonpans. The salt was then used to preserve the fish, mainly herring, which was exported to the low countries. Much of the architecture along the Firth of Forth reflects a Dutch influence and the many conical turrets on the bigger houses are a testament to the French connection. Although whisky is considered our national drink, it was French claret that was most commonly drunk amongst the well-to-do in the 16th, 17th and 18th centuries. Whisky only became a malt-derived drink in the mid-1700s and did not enjoy its international popularity until the late 19th century when it was made available in blended form.

Scots speech has retained a collection of French words such as stank for drain or pool (Old French, estanc); boule for marble or ashet for a large meat plate (French, assiette). Scots also seem to have a great warmth for European nations who beat England at football. Probably the strong affinity with foreign parts is because Scotland, like Ireland, has a long history of emigration. The English view of abroad was more that of coloniser while the Scots migrant's interest was the attainment of a better life.

Q: YOU SAID THE IRISH JOINED THE EURO. HOW DOES THIS AFFECT NORTHERN IRELAND?

A: The border between Northern Ireland and the Republic has presented endless problems to both the British and the Irish governments since this very arbitrary line was drawn in the early 1920s. When Ireland broke the link with the pound Sterling and adopted the Punt there were then two currencies in a tiny island with a pre-Euro difference of some 25% between them — the UK pound equating roughly IR£1.25. So the people of the island of Ireland are used to dealing with a rate of exchange. No great trauma there.

What seems certain to be affected is tourist revenue on both sides of the border. Logically, holidaymakers from mainland Europe will find Ireland more attractive with everything priced in Euros just like at home. But they may just stop short of visiting Northern Ireland if it means changing money and all the concomitant calculations with every purchase. Not that Britain cares overmuch for its Irish province but a pro-Euro lobby from that quarter may influence the UK parliament in hastening the introduction of the European currency. Further pressure will develop through Ireland's acceptance of European fiscal policies that have produced many lower priced commodities south of the border; petrol being one glaring example.

Q: SO THE UK MAY OPT FOR THE EURO?

A: Possibly, although it will really be up to the people and not the government. Tony Blair's New Labour party initially seemed to sit on the fence, probably not wishing to alienate the more conservative voter. After allowing free rein to the pro-Euro voices, they are now in a second term of office with no real opposition to prevent a third term. Blair has always maintained the position that there will be a referendum on the Euro after the five conditions of convergence have been met, but only one has been achieved as we go to press. A referendum on this issue is still a long way off.

Q: What will happen to Northern Ireland if Scotland becomes independent?

A: That's a very tough question. The settlers of the Northern Ireland Plantation dating back to the 16th Century, were mainly of Scottish origin. The Northern Ireland telephone directory is full of Scottish, largely Lowland, names, such as Ramsay, Barr, Ferguson, Craig, Orr and many others. The affinity between Northern Irish Unionists and Scotland is strong both in bloodline and in the shared Presbyterian faith. The Americans coined the term Scots-Irish to distinguish them from the aboriginal Irish. A modern paradox is that while the Northern Irish Unionists bang the Lambeg drum to proclaim their undying (and unreciprocated) loyalty to the British state, in Scotland at least one third of Scots are Nationalists who vote for independence from the British state.

In the lexicon of descriptive words used in Northern Ireland, one has to be extraordinarily wary of the terms used. Derry is the original Irish town name while the Unionists prefer Londonderry. The mainland is used by Unionists to describe Britain as might the people of the Isle of Wight; Nationalists would neither use the term nor have the mindset to even think in that way. Nationalist and Republican are words used by Unionists to describe 'them'. The Scots-Irish go to great lengths to show their loyalty to Britain and their devotion to the Queen. Yet in a recent poll in Scotland 25% were in favour of scrapping the monarchy, making them republicans per se, while 35% support the SNP and independence.

Q: So if the UK is no more, where do the Northern Irish stand?

A: If Scottish nationalism and, by extension, republicanism continue to grow, it is not unreasonable to deduce that an independent Scottish republic would be inevitable. This could produce the anomalous situation where Northern Ireland would continue to salute the Union Flag and pay homage to the British Monarch while the Unionists' own kith and kin in Scotland, just across the water, became citizens of a foreign country on a par with citizens of the Irish Republic. So, if Scotland opted for both independence and republicanism, the United Kingdom could no longer exist simply because the original union – that of the Crowns of England and Scotland under James VI – would be dissolved. Northern Ireland would then pay fealty to London and the English Parliament while their blood brothers and sisters only a few miles to the east became an independent nation.

The Establishment old guard shudder at the ramifications of an independent Scotland. A further complication is that the Scots-Irish are losing what has been described as 'the numbers game'.

Q: WHAT'S THE 'NUMBERS GAME'?

A: It is the N I population split between Unionist and Nationalist. When the Six Counties of Ulster became the state of Northern Ireland in 1922, the population was split roughly 60/40 in favour of the Unionists. The entire nine counties of Ulster would have comprised Northern Ireland – but – had the excluded three counties of Donegal, Monaghan and Cavan been made part of Northern Ireland the balance of population would have been in the Nationalists favour. Hence the confusion between Ulster and Northern Ireland. All N I counties are in Ulster but not all the counties of Ulster are in Northern Ireland. This, incidentally, was one of the reasons why the Royal Ulster Constabulary changed its name to the Police Service of Northern Ireland. The 60/40 split has slowly leavened to near parity.

Why?

One reason was because the vast majority of the Nationalists were Catholic and many followed the RC church's teaching on birth control, so the Catholics were out-breeding the Protestants. Another factor was what has been unkindly referred to as the chicken run, a term coined by white South Africans and Zimbabweans to describe those who fled Africa when these countries achieved black majority rule. Some Protestant families had endured enough of the bloodshed and, not unreasonably, decided to relocate to Britain or even further afield. In fairness there were also Catholic families who opted for a more peaceful existence, however 'the numbers game', as many Protestants saw it, was being lost. The population split is now pretty static as the Catholic Church's doctrinaire line on birth control is invariably ignored by Catholic families.

Q: IF THE SPLIT REACHES 50/50 COULD IT GO EITHER WAY?

A: Like so many aspects of life in N I it is not quite that simple. There has always been a small percentage of N I Catholics who have no problem being British. How big a percentage no-one knows because not too many Catholics will announce in the local pub that they are voting Unionist.

Why would they want to be British?

It is important to remember that the latest 'Troubles' began in 1969, not from a resurgence of nationalism, not from a love of republicanism nor a hatred of Britain; the infamous 1969 Burntollet March was driven by a demand for equal civil rights. As a simple analogy, the black civil rights marchers in the USA didn't want dominance or African rule, they simply wanted to be treated as equal citizens in their own country. Many of the Catholic marchers were not concerned about whose flag flew over the Town Hall, they wanted equality in jobs, council housing allocation and an end to any form of discrimination. Many county councils were 100% Protestant-staffed, as was the Harland and Woolf shipyard, as was (and still largely is) the police force.

Similarly, the march in 1972 where the British Army shot dead 13 men and wounded many others, was not a 'Brits Out' march, it too was a civil rights protest march. Alas, it was the fury and outrage engendered by 'Bloody Sunday' which drove so many young men into the arms of the IRA and its splinter groups. Britain's introduction of internment without trial and the parachute regiment's action on Bloody Sunday probably contributed more to the violence and bloodshed in Northern Ireland than any amount of latent nationalism.

Q: OKAY, BUT SAY THE SHIFT WENT TO 60/40 IN FAVOUR OF THE NATIONALISTS.

A: Should the shift be that definite, then in all probability a re-united Ireland would be inevitable though it would probably be less traumatic than feared. The conceptual barriers may remain and the knee-jerk reaction to a united Ireland will take time to die but many of the great barriers to Ulster Protestants no longer exist.

Such as?

Britain was once much richer than Ireland. British welfare payments were much higher than Irish ones. The British National Health Service used to be the envy of the world while the Irish people had to pay for health care. Irish salaries were lower and emigration was a cause for national shame. The Protestant slogan, 'Home Rule is Rome Rule', was largely true with the Catholic Church manipulating far too many aspects of Irish life. Contraception, which Northern Ireland took for granted, was forbidden in Ireland and contraceptives only went on sale there in 1985. Books and magazines were banned with the sweep of an Archbishop's blue pencil. Cases of discrimination against Protestants, though nowhere on the scale of the reverse in the North, were not uncommon.

Now with the influence of the European Union, the Irish economy has boomed, salaries are higher, Irish jobs are being advertised in the British press, welfare payments have risen, allowances for pensioners and the disabled now exceed the British equivalent, many prices are cheaper and petrol is closer to the European rate than the exorbitant UK one. The RC church in Ireland has had its iron grip prised away finger by finger, mainly through self-inflicted injuries. Sadly the conceptual barriers will be the last to fall. More's the pity, because anyone who has lived on either side of the border will affirm that the Northern Irish Unionist has a philosophical disposition much more in tune with his southern cousin than with the natives of London's Home Counties.

Q: DO THE IRISH PEOPLE WANT NORTHERN IRELAND BACK?

A: Theoretically yes. The whole ethos of the Irish Republic was the extrication of the island of Ireland from British control. The establishment of The Irish Free State gave 26 counties of Ireland autonomy but Britain retained the north-eastern six counties. Irish people always tended to refer to 'the six counties' rather like six relatives who had gone abroad but were still very much part of the family. The main political parties all paid lip service to the restoration of the six counties and a re-united Ireland. So much for the theory, but there are many Irish people who dread the idea of a re-united Ireland. They tend to see the Northern Irish Protestants as a rather truculent, abrasive and humourless bunch and feel that the problems of the North should remain a British problem. Some argue that Ireland can live without nearly a million hostile Protestants creating friction in the north east corner of the island.

Q: WHAT WILL HAPPEN TO THE COMMONWEALTH WHEN THE QUEEN DIES?

A: No-one can be sure how each individual nation will react. When Elizabeth became Queen in 1952, the old trappings of empire and colonialism were still very much in place. She was head of the then British Commonwealth and in Whitehall there was still a Colonial Office. As the colonial grip was prised open, one nation after another, and each former colony became an independent country, virtually all the new nations saw some benefit in retaining a commonwealth link, as ex-pupils might attend old school reunions. The queen remained as the titular head of the Commonwealth (the British bit having been dropped), primarily because she was in situ during the transition and nobody could think of a better idea. Whether the member countries would accept the concept of a hereditary replacement after the queen dies is hard to forecast. In theory, with the great majority of all the member states being democratic republics with an elected head of state, it seems unlikely that an unelected, hereditary prince would be their choice. On the other hand, it might be the very difference of Charles' status which might make him acceptable.

57

Q: WHY HAVE YOU BEEN GOING ON SO MUCH ABOUT THE IRISH? I THOUGHT WE WERE DISCUSSING SCOTLAND?

A: I get a little distracted sometimes and with my Irish background I tend to go off on tangents. But the point is that all the nations in Great Britain are linked by far more than simple geography, especially the affinity between Scotland and the North of Ireland, and our discussion in this chapter shows this.

CHAPTER 3
SEEING AND DOING

Q: WHY ARE THERE THE SAME SORT OF TOURIST BOOKS IN EVERY BOOKSHOP IN SCOTLAND?

A: I think what you are referring to is the preponderence of a certain type of book that is often stocked in tourist information centres and the like. It is simply because most of these types of outlet are stocked by a supplier who takes the hassle factor away from the retailer by managing the stocks of books themselves. The downside is that the supplier then loads the shelves with items that have a proven sales record and are frequently even published by the said supplier.

Q: SO MORE PROFIT FOR THE SUPPLIER?

A: Absolutely ... and less choice for the customer. Historic Scotland have recently been taken to task about this issue and seem to be gradually realising that they need to change what they stock to create a more level playing field for publishers in Scotland. If you need to see a greater range of books then take a saunter during your travels into any of the big chains or large independent bookshops such as WHSmith, Ottakars, Borders, Waterstones and that marvellous cultural oasis the Ceilidh Place in Ullapool.

Q: SO WILL I BE ABLE TO BUY THIS BOOK IN A TOURIST INFORMATION CENTRE?

A: So long as they have not taken offence to your first question!

Q: DOES THE LOCH NESS MONSTER EXIST?

A: Of course it does. Do you really think that intelligent, educated men and women of science would station themselves along the banks of the loch from Inverness to Fort Augustus in expectation of a sighting if no such animal existed? Do you imagine that tourists from all over the world would flock to The Great Glen if their journey was thought to be in vain? Would serious zoologists plumb the loch with echo-sounders and the latest sonar equipment if Nessie's appearance was not a possibility? Just because the only photograph of this wondrous beast turned out to be a hoax, there is no reason to question the faith of so many, especially the Highland shop-keepers and tour operators. One remarkable aspect of Nessie is her consistency. Sightings of her always occur in the early Spring — must be something to do with the clarity of the air.

Q: THE TOURIST PLUGS ALL INCLUDE PLACES LIKE EDINBURGH, STIRLING, LOCH LOMOND, BURNS COUNTRY ETC. WHERE ELSE IS WORTH VISITING?

A: Kipling penned the thought, 'What should they know of England who only England know?' It could be applied to tourism. What do they know of Scotland who only Edinburgh know. Sure, tours of historic places like Edinburgh are essential for the visitor but the risk is too narrow a picture. However, no visit to Scotland would be complete without a visit to Edinburgh.

Princes Street, although awash with standard anytown stores, is still stunning and the view across Princes Street Gardens to the Old Town remains one of the finest in any capital city in the world.

Q: WHAT'S THE DIFFERENCE BETWEEN THE OLD TOWN AND THE NEW TOWN?

A: There has been a settlement on the Castle Rock since it was occupied by the ancient Picts, who called it Dunedin. The oldest surviving building is St Margaret's Chapel, located inside the castle walls which was built in the 11th century. Because of the constraints of fortification the only way to build was up – or in the case of some of the older closes – down.

Down?

Yes, because of the lack of space, some closes were developed by tunnelling under the surface of the main street, now known as The Royal Mile. Because of a lack of sanitation and the spread of disease some of these 'under-streets' such as Mary King's Close were sealed off and not rediscovered until the early 1980s.

The Old Town spread northwards over the Nor' Loch (now Princes St Gardens) for three reasons. First: there was simply not enough space to contain the growing number of Edinburgh's population. Second: the lack of sanitation and the consequent spread of disease was rendering the Old Town almost uninhabitable, and third: after the Act of Union of 1707 when Scotland and England (and Wales!) became one country there was no need for the fortifications which surrounded the Old Town. In 1767 a competition was held for a street plan for the proposed New Town. James Craig, just a lad of 23, won the competition and the structure of the New Town is accredited to him.

Q: THE NEW TOWN STREET NAMES AREN'T VERY SCOTTISH?

A: Well spotted, they are not. After the failed Jacobite Rising of 1745 when Bonnie Prince Charlie almost succeeded in reclaiming the throne for the Stewarts, the city fathers of Edinburgh (and Glasgow) were at pains to show their allegiance to the Hanoverian monarchy. The three main east/west thoroughfares George St, Princes St and Queen St all allude to the Hanovarian dynasty as do Charlotte Square, Hanover St, Frederick St, Saxe-Coburg Place, Cumberland St, and Great King St. In Glasgow the main square was named George Square. Now that the need for such obeisance has passed, many letter writers to the Scottish press are asking if the city could have a little less commemoration of the Germans and a little more of Wallace, Bruce, Burns and a host of the Scottish scientists, engineers, philosophers and medical men who contributed so much to society as a whole.

Q: WHERE SHOULD I BEGIN AN EDINBURGH TOUR?

A: Go to the top of Calton Hill, just a brief walk east from Waverley Station. From there you can make a short circular walk, taking in views of Arthur's Seat in Holyrood Park, the Old Town, Princes St, the New Town, the Forth Bridges, the Firth of Forth, Leith and a fine view east out to North Berwick Law and East Lothian. Alternatively, go into Holyrood Park and take the circular route round Arthur's Seat.

For a brief overview of the city you won't find a better introduction. Another option is the open-topped bus tours which leave from Waverley Station at regular intervals. If you are lucky your guide might be the knowledgeable and entertaining Robert Leslie.

Once you've seen all the landmarks in quick time you can then plan your itinerary for a more leisurely tour.

Q: SHOULD I GO TO GLASGOW?

A: You must. Compare the rather prim, and preserved Edinburgh with the bustling, brash and brimful streets of Glasgow. Edinburgh recoils from neon or projecting signs of more than 18 inches; it feels faint at the thought of a motorway; its skyline remains as restrained as a century ago — apart, of course, from those peripheral areas where the proletariat have been decanted and tower blocks prevail. Craig's architecturally stunning New Town can be a little like a museum.

Q: WHAT'S SO GOOD ABOUT GLASGOW?

A: Contrast Glasgow's skyline with sedate Edinburgh, note the mix of architecture and the old, side by side with the new. When they renovate a building in Glasgow city centre they hang the world's largest advertising banners from the scaffolding! Walk along Argyle St, up Buchanan St into Sauchiehall St. Edinburgh has Princes St and a few purpose-built shopping centres like The Gyle and The Fort but Glasgow has heart and soul. Talk to the people. Ask them directions. And if they don't know they'll grab hold of passing pedestrians and ask them. Edinburgh is polite but Glasgow is more than polite, it has warmth. Marvel at the M8 motorway driven through the city centre and over the Clyde. You want history? Go to Glasgow Cathedral, learn the history of St Kentigern (aka St Mungo). Ask the wonderfully friendly and informative staff to explain the Glasgow crest with the tree, the ring, the fish and the bird. Examine the sacristy door with its bullet holes reflecting a more turbulent age. See Kentigern's tomb in the crypt.

If you have any awe left, cross the courtyard and enter the Museum of Religion where all the major faiths of the world are featured. Pause and wonder at Salvador Dali's Crucifixion of Christ of St John of the Cross. Across the road, visit the oldest house in Glasgow, once a cathedral property for senior clergy, now a small museum, Provand's Lordship. Almost next door is the massive Royal Infirmary built at the end of Victoria's reign and reflecting all the wealth, confidence and splendour of Glasgow as The Second City of the Empire. Behind it, stroll up to the Necropolis, that gothic monument to man's vanity where the great and good were buried, having insisted on huge, ornate tombs to remind people just how great and good they were.

And we've only begun: the Museum of Transport where Partick meets the River Kelvin is an absolute must for all ages and nationalities; go in the main door and turn left to see the most wonderful re-creation of a 1930's cobbled street with cars of the period parked either side; pause at the cake shop with prices all of the period, the chemist, the pub, the little cinema (go in and take a seat in the one-and-nines and watch a movie on Glasgow), the electric shop with 1930's hoovers and electric kettles; don't miss the subway station, see the actual 'tube' trains of the period complete with 'no spitting' signs. Leave the 1930s street and wander amongst all the vintage cars, fire engines, trains (including the royal train) trams, buses, motor bikes, cop cars, horse-drawn vehicles and caravans. If you are not exhausted with such an immense array of early transport go upstairs – in fact begin upstairs – and see the story of the Clyde and its ships. At one time 96% of all the ships at sea were Clyde-built. Examine the flawless models, note the precise detail from stem to stern, from the rigging in the masts to the Plimsoll line below — absolutely stunning. If you run low on energy, sit and watch the video story of the Clyde shipyards.

Q: WHAT ABOUT ART?

A: If it was not closed for refurbishment I would tell you to cross the road from the Transport Museum to the magnificent Kelvingrove Museum which contains a superb natural history section. Paintings by most of Scotland's best known artists including Raeburn, the Glasgow Boys and the Colourists are here as are works by Reubens, Turner, Rembrandt, Lowry, Whistler and some of the medieval Italians. During the refurbishment most of these can be seen at the McLennan Galleries in Sauchiehall St. Don't be misled by the unpretentious entrance of the McLennan, it is stunning inside.

There is also the Gallery of Modern Art at Royal Exchange Square and Charles Rennie Mackintosh's Willow Tea Rooms in Sauchiehall St. A visit to Glasgow University, founded in 1451, is well worth the trip and it also houses the Hunterian Museum which focuses on natural history and contains a splendid display of fossils, ancient artifacts and relics of Roman Britain.

On the south side of the river the famous Burrell Collection is contained within a bespoke building in the grounds of Pollok Park. Glasgow City Council have a policy that museums are for the benefit of the people and consequently no entry charges are made; all Glasgow museums are free. So it is certainly no mean city, it is a generous, big-hearted city.

Q: WHAT IS THE 'NO MEAN CITY' REPUTATION?

A: It is surprising you've heard of that, as the term is very dated. Alas, the image created by this book about the razor gang violence of post-war Glasgow has taken a long time to die. Sure, Glasgow may have been to Scotland what Chicago was to the US and perhaps there are corners of Chicago, or any city, which might be wiser to avoid, but a visit is well worth the trip.

Q: WHY ARE EDINBURGH AND GLASGOW SO DIFFERENT?

A: Evolution. When Edinburgh became Scotland's capital, Glasgow was a relatively small town on the River Clyde. Though its cathedral was founded in the 12th century and its University in 1451 it was only in the 18th and 19th centuries that Glasgow began to expand rapidly. The coal, steel, shipbuilding and textile industries swelled the city's population to over a million, drawing in workers from the land, from the Highlands and from Ireland. Edinburgh's evolution was quite different; the capital was historically the centre for law, the church, the parliament, education, medicine, literature, the arts and more recently the world famous Edinburgh Festival of theatre, opera, music and dance. Consequently Edinburgh acquired the reputation for refinement and, from a Glasgow view, snobbery.

This veneer has long been mocked by Glaswegians as all 'fur coat and nae knickers' or all 'kippers and curtains', this latter aside alluding to the fact that behind those ornate curtains there lay quite modest fare, the former being self-explanatory. Because of Glasgow's in-your-face, down to earth focus on metal bashing and honest toil Edinburgh folk felt themselves just that bit superior. Two rival car stickers (derived from I LOVE NY) said it all. In the late 1980s Glasgow, under its master of PR, Harry Diamond, utilised John Struthers's brilliant slogan 'Glasgowsmiles Better'. Edinburgh responded with a nice touch of self-mockery with, 'Edinburgh's slightly superior'.

Q: IS THE RIVALRY SERIOUS?

A: Not very. There is surprisingly little interchange other than amongst the professional classes. A sense of remoteness tends to prevail. Scottish media person, Muriel Gray, once wrote, 'the greatest distance between any two cities is the distance between Glasgow and Edinburgh'. Many citizens of both cities have not visited the other, apart from possibly a football outing.

There is a degree of resentment in Glasgow towards Edinburgh's privileged position. For a start, the capital is topographically and architecturally very beautiful. It has the history, the castle, the Royal Mile, Holyrood Palace, Arthur's Seat, Calton Hill, Princes St, the New Town and it attracts tourists in their millions. It is awash with hotels, B&Bs, restaurants, pubs, city tours, gardens, all in a much greater proportion to Glasgow. Many people felt that when Scotland re-established its own parliament that it should have been sited in Perth, Stirling or Glasgow but no, it went to fat, over-endowed Edinburgh. A further cause of resentment was when the Royal Yacht **Britannia** was paid off and retired. Many argued it should have gone home to the Clyde where it was built, but no, it went to Edinburgh where it comprises yet one more major tourist attraction.

Q: YOU MENTIONED THE EDINBURGH INTERNATIONAL FESTIVAL?

A: Edinburgh's Festival alone attracts visitors numbering in excess of the city's population. Or to be more precise, Festivals, because what began as the Theatre Festival just after WWII extended to the Festival Fringe, the Film Festival, the TV Festival, the Jazz Festival, the Book Festival and the Military Tattoo — all bringing in vast amounts of revenue to an already affluent city. Even the winter brings in great numbers of visitors for the Hogmanay Party with its funfair, concerts and fireworks.

Q: WHAT IS THE FESTIVAL FRINGE?

A: In the early days of the Edinburgh Festival, it was all a rather highbrow event with many people in evening dress walking the streets of Edinburgh to or from one venue or another. The general perception was that the Festival was elitist and snobby. The Festival Fringe grew up around the Festival featuring many new plays, the avant garde, comedy and often anti-establishment material. The Fringe now comprises many more performances than the official Festival ever did.

Q: WHAT SCENIC AREAS SHOULD I VISIT?

A: The Highlands and Islands unquestionably hold some of the loveliest places on the planet. Scotland has only five million inhabitants and most of them are centred in a corridor from the Firth of Forth through to the Firth of Clyde. The greatest population density is found in the conurbations of Glasgow and greater Lanarkshire through the midlands to Edinburgh and East Lothian. Beyond the central belt and Stirling there are only three other cities: Dundee, Aberdeen and Inverness. Perth (still a town) for example, has a population of only 45,000 which equates to just one housing scheme on the periphery of Glasgow.

The remainder of Scotland is, by English standards, empty. There are more roads within a radius of 20 miles from Manchester than in the entire area of the Highlands and Islands of Scotland. If the road from Glenshee to Braemar was blocked, the round trip via Stonehaven would span roughly 200 miles which is half the distance from Edinburgh to London. On a walking holiday one can walk all day and never meet another soul. If you have the time, get out and explore the rest of Scotland. The list of places to go is too long for the likes of this book but the West Coast and the Hebrides takes some beating especially when the sun is shining. And where better to be at the end of each May than in Islay during the festival of Malt and Music. And let's not forget Scotland's best kept secret.

Q: WHAT IS SCOTLAND'S BEST KEPT SECRET?

A: It is a common term used to describe the areas that visitors pass through as they gallop blinkered to the watering holes of Edinburgh and Glasgow. If they fly into Glasgow, Prestwick or Edinburgh, they pass right over the top of the region. It encompasses Dumfries and Galloway and the Scottish Borders and stretches from Stranraer in the west to Berwick-upon-Tweed in the east. For scenery, tourists automatically head north. The English will drive up via the M6 in the west or the A1 in the east. The more adventurous will choose the A7, A701 or A702 through the rolling magnificence of the Borders, though the great majority of visitors will miss most of the Borders and all of Dumfries and Galloway

Not unreasonably the attractions of Edinburgh Castle, Stirling Castle, Loch Katrine, The Trossachs, Glencoe and the many other areas of great beauty or historic interest, are the focus of most visitors but Southern Scotland is awash with castles, rivers, lochs, burns and hills that roll on forever. It has everything the famous English Lake District has but much more of it, with none of the overcrowding Windermere and Ullswater experience. The key to the eastern part of Southern Scotland is the River Tweed which rises just north of the Dumfriesshire town of Moffat and not far from where the Clyde and Annan begin their journeys to the sea. The Tweed soon flows past Tweedsmuir where the author John Buchan was born. It carries on eastward linking all the prominent towns in the Borders — Peebles, Galashiels, Melrose (in whose abbey Wallace's heart was buried), Dryburgh, Kelso, Coldstream then enters the sea at historic Berwick. For the western part, think of Ireland and rolling farmland, expansive uplands, vast sandy bays rich in wildfowl and netted salmon and enchanting sma' glens high in the hills.

Q: Any recommendations?

A: It really does depend on your interests. Many visitors from the English-speaking New World are keen to trace their ancestry. Some have been inspired by a movie they've seen, whilst many, especially the Japanese, will endure a 12-hour (or longer) day trip to gaze upon Loch Ness. They stoically hide their disappointment at the non-appearance of Nessie, the monster. On a coach trip to St Andrews it is not uncommon to find the passengers evenly split between those who wish to visit the shrine of Golf, the Old Course, those who are keen to trace the path of The Reformation, or even those hopeful of a glimpse of the second-in-line to the throne. Many wish to see Loch Lomond simply because they know the Bonnie Bonnie Banks lyric of the famous song. Others are interested in the Roman fort at Drymen and the Antonine Wall which ran from the Firth of Clyde to the Firth of Forth. The Antonine wall was abandoned by the Romans as they simply could not contain the belligerent aboriginals, so they withdrew to the south and built Hadrian's Wall from Carlisle to Wallsend near Newcastle. Loch Lomond is steeped in history from the Romans to the Celts, the Irish missionaries and the Vikings who hauled their boats from the sea loch overland at Arrocahar to Tarbet and onto the waters of the Loch.

Some visitors like statistics. Loch Lomond is the longest and largest freshwater loch at 18.5km and 71.1km^2 respectively, while Loch Morar is the deepest freshwater loch at 310m making it the 17th deepest in the world. Some may have the name Colquhoun or Lennox in the family and want to see the family's roots at Luss. Similarly, the MacGregors were the big cheeses to the north of the loch while the Buchanans ruled the roost to the east. Keen walkers will want to do the incomparably beautiful West Highland Way beginning at Milngavie near Loch Lomond and stretching roughly 100 miles north to Fort William.

Q: Why were the battles of Falkirk, Stirling Bridge and Bannockburn so close together?

A: Any English army marching on Scotland would travel up the east coast primarily because the terrain was less hostile than the west. This made the northern Border town of Berwick-on-Tweed of great strategic importance. It changed ownership no fewer than 14 times between the 13th and 16th centuries. Around Berwick and north to Edinburgh there are many battlefield sites such as Flodden, Dunbar and Prestonpans. There are castles at Alnwick, Berwick, Dunbar, Tantallon, Hailes, Dirleton and Edinburgh along with several others further inland. To an invader, taking Edinburgh and the borderlands would be the beginning. The next step would be to cross the Firth of Forth and carry on northwards. Armies crossing water are vulnerable, so an invading army would head towards the narrowest point of the Firth of Forth which is the bridge at Stirling. En route to Stirling lie Falkirk and Bannockburn hence the battlefield sites. An invader intent on taking Scotland would have to hold Stirling. The castle was once the seat of the Scottish kings and was the first home of the Scottish Parliament in 1326. Both Mary Queen of Scots and her son James VI were crowned there as infants.

One visit to Stirling Castle will confirm its strategic importance. It is a mighty fortress built on solid dolerite that rises above the town and is master of all it surveys. You'll notice that the Wallace monument nearby has an uncanny resemblance to Mel Gibson!

Q: HOW COME HIGHLAND SPEECH IS CLEARER THAN LOWLAND?

A: There used to be a common saying that the best English was spoken in Inverness and Dublin.

In Ireland and the Highlands of Scotland the native tongue of the people was Gaelic (pronounced Gaylic in Ireland and Gallic – rhyming with phallic – in Scotland). Because of the Penal Laws in Ireland and after the 1745 Rebellion in Scotland, the English language began to predominate. As the Gaelic and English languages had nothing in common, the Irish and the Highlander learned English in a very pure, undiluted form. The accents are distinctly regional as are some of the vernacular terms that have been translated directly from the Gaelic to the English. The Irish for example will say, 'I am after having my tea,' which is grammatically odd in English but is a direct translation from the Irish Gaelic structure. Similarly, Highlanders will ask each other if they're 'speaking the Gaelic'. Apart from these idiosyncratic touches, the English was pure.

Q: WE FIND HIGHLAND SPEECH ACTUALLY CLEARER TO UNDERSTAND THAN SOME OF THE ENGLISH ACCENTS, WHY SO?

A: In some respects it is purer than Standard English which became affected and sloppy over time. In the English Home Counties, the H is no longer pronounced in WH words. Words such as while, whether, whet, where or which, are pronounced wile, weather, wet, were and witch. Nor is the H pronounced in abhorrent or adhesive. The R has disappeared from all word endings such as, butter, bitter, winter, super and many others, apart from in the SW of England where the people of Cornwall, Somerset and Devon steadfastly retain the R. The trend has crept into commercial names such as SupaSava, BettaBuys or SavaCenta. Pura is the brand name of a Shell diesel fuel. The southerners counter with the view that the Scots 'roll their Rs'. In Edwardian times there was even an upper-class affectation of mispronouncing Rs as Ws so converting 'break bread' into 'bweak bwead'. Many of the breed (bweed?) still choose to mispronounce 'gone off' as 'gorn orf'. Though clearly incorrect it acts as a shibboleth to indicate upper-class breeding. The only other group of English speakers who adopt this affectation are the Cockneys. Oddly the English put rogue Rs into other words such as drawring, Indiar, Canadar and sawr. The aristocrat prime minister of the 1960s, Alec Douglas-Home (pronounced Hume), in a speech once alluded to 'flower power' only it sounded like 'flah pah' which ironically is precisely how the Cockney would say it only with a slightly shorter 'a'.

Q: BUT ISN'T THE OBJECT OF COMMUNICATION TO BE UNDERSTOOD?

A: Of course. No-one could misinterpret a request for a glass of 'wahta' but there are times when mispronunciation can mislead the listener. For example, making homophones out of more and moor, shore and sure, pore and poor, tore and tour, or when a radio presenter says that the next programme is about 'Wales' and the listener is unsure if that means large sea mammals or the land of the leek and daffodil.

The Irish and the Highlander (and in this instance, the Scots in general) would always pronounce their WHs and their Rs (listen to TV's Taggart characters say 'there's been a murder'). 'Murder' in Surrey sounds like 'muhdah'. Condensing words is another southern speech distortion rendering the syllables mouth and shire in Portsmouth, Hampshire as muth and sha — so Monmouthshire is pronounced Monmuthsha and Perthshire more like Persia. Whole syllables can be discarded making the five syllabled word 'particularly' sound like 'p'tickley' and 'perhaps' as 'p'aps'. The former Tory deputy prime minister Willie Whitelaw had dreadfully affected speech patterns which made him almost incomprehensible. A word such as 'secretary' would be cut down to 'secry' (Whitelaw was a Scot but a landed one who did not talk like his tenants).

These distortions are spreading, even to Scotland, but one sound remains uniquely southern — the affected pronunciation of the letter 'O' which is not only alien to northern and Celtic ears but to every language on earth. The French, Italian, Spanish, American, Irish, Scots and northern English pronunciation of 'no' is identical. It is only the Queen's English which makes it so prolonged and artificial. The extended 'a' is another southern distortion. While all the world pronounces 'castle' as rhyming with 'hassle', the southern version is 'cawsell' and when all the world's media were discussing Iraq (rhyming with attack), most of the London BBC stuck with Irawq with notable exceptions such as Scotsman James Naughtie and Welshman John Humphries.

So when American visitors, for example, say they find Highland speech so clear, it is because the Highlander, like the American, pronounces his Rs and WHs but, more importantly, he uses no Lowland syntax. Outside the Highlands the Scots, Doric or Lallans were the native tongues of a great swathe of Scotland from Aberdeen south to the Borders. Their roots had much in common with English roots so a non-Scot reading Burns might think he was reading bad English. The Doric terms loons and quines for men and women may sound like a foreign language but they were used by Shakespeare and later fell into disuse in common English.

The Scots use of 'mind' for 'remember' sounds quaint to English ears but it is a perfectly good English word, as is 'aye' for 'yes', still used in Northern England and in the Houses of Parliament to vote. 'Cannae', 'wouldnae', 'didnae', 'shouldnae' are all valid Lowland terms. Rapid Lanarkshire speech such as 'Ah'm no gonny dae it' (with a glottal stop dropped 't') can be difficult for visitors to catch. 'Gonny' and 'didnae' are not indigenous to Highland speech nor are many Scots words which pepper most Lowland verbal exchanges. Also, with the Highlands having an extremely low population density, speech tends to be much slower than in the urban Lowlands so the three factors combined – pure English, slower delivery and a mellifluous accent – give Highland speech its reputation for clarity.

Q: AM I WRONG OR DO THE SCOTS SWEAR A LOT?

A: No you are quite correct, the use of swear words is common and widespread. The Brits don't really expect the middle classes to swear. Had John Major or Tony Blair produced the infamous Nixon Tapes, the people would have been aghast. John Major managed a Richter Scale tremor before his election defeat in 1997 when he referred, not unreasonably, to those who had plotted against him as 'bastards'.

The middle classes will generally use expletives to describe an emotion, enhance a story or for exaggerated emphasis. The working-class man (and many women for that matter) use swear words as a matter of course as though it were part of the local idiom.

The class association is more pronounced in England where

people are much more self-conscious about such divisions. The aristocracy had no problem with this. The Duke of Barchester can state baldly that 'the man is a complete cunt' and nobody seems to mind. He may even attract approval from the deferential as being 'a real character'. Lesser mortals would not gain such approval.

Q: IS THERE MUCH SWEARING ON BRITISH TV?

A: There is a demarcation called the nine o'clock watershed which means that after that hour more adult viewing can be screened. Some of the anomalies in this field would confuse any visitor. The word 'fuck' is still taboo in most situations, however the word 'bugger' causes no offence and is almost a term of endearment. Precisely the same associations apply to the word 'sod'. 'The poor sod crashed his car', is a comment which would evoke only sympathy from the British. Why buggery and sodomy should be wholly acceptable to a nation which can be horrified by fucking is a sociological phenomenon which merits a separate analysis.

The word 'bloody' caused offence because it was a corruption of 'by Our Lady'. Like so many corruptions such as 'crikey' or 'cripes' (Christ), 'heck' (hell), 'cor blimey' (God blind me), 'lor'' (lord), 'by gad' or 'by gum', the word 'bloody' had a religious root so an alternative evolved in 'bleedin''. As it was the Cockney or working-class folk who opted for 'bleedin'', the middle classes retained the technically more blasphemous 'bloody'. The roots are now forgotten but the bourgeoisie can be heard admonishing their children, 'Don't say 'bleedin'' dear, it's not nice'. In fact, the word is wholly innocuous, it is the associations that matter.

'Prick' or 'dick' are generally considered quite inoffensive whilst the female equivalent remains public enemy No 1, but it is all fashion. For example, in Spain the use of the word for the female genitalia, coño, bears none of the horror it might evoke in Britain; moreover, Spanish parents may use the word as a term of affection with children. Other terms such as beaver, pussy or fanny cause little offence. There are cultural and national pitfalls to be wary of. If an American woman said she had a very sore or itchy fanny she could not use the phrase with the same ease in the UK as in the US where it means bottom. Similarly, the American husband who informed the dinner table that he had had to rub liniment into his wife's fanny after a long day's cycling would have received sympathetic and supportive smiles back home in Pittsburgh but he would be most surprised by the disbelieving looks of fellow diners in Perthshire.

Q: HOW ABOUT FOUR LETTER WORDS IN PRINT?

A: Interestingly enough our press gets in a real tangle over swear words. While four letter words can be heard on radio and TV, the press still can't quite get to grips with this extremely common form of vernacular speech. On the one hand it will print the most intimate and unpleasant details of some dreadful rape or murder yet in an adjacent column it will print a courtroom extract such as, 'He told me to f*** off' 'And why did he tell you to f*** off?' 'Because he said I was a right c***' 'And what did you reply?' 'I told him he was a right c*** as well and he was talking b*******'. This ludicrous coyness is both hilarious and pointless. If the reader did not know what the words were, then the report becomes incomprehensible, yet the asterisks indicate that the words are self-evident — so if they are self-evident why adopt these shrinking violet disguises.

One idiotic defence was that children might read them. If children are mature enough to read newspapers, great. So let them read about the world and all its degrading facets. The unworldly should stand outside a school fast-food or confectionery shop at lunchtime. The language used by boys and girls as they carry out their angelic little exchanges would leave one in no doubt that their vocabularies are not lacking one whit in the swearing department.

Q: ANY OTHER SPEECH DIFFERENCES TO WATCH OUT FOR?

A: You might on occasion be confused by what could be called football grammar, used, often in the West of Scotland, by team managers and players when commenting on the game. 'The ball could've went into the net' or 'should've went into the goal' is not really bad grammar; it is idiomatic, as is 'hopefully we'll get a result'.

Q: ANY SERIOUS LANGUAGE PITFALLS?

A: Not really. As with most things in life, people are judged by their manners and their actions. Offence is seldom taken where no offence is meant. Americans should be aware that the British expression 'dying for a fag' has no gay connotation. Australians may get a funny look in British stationery stores when they ask for Durex which here is called Sellotape (or Scotch tape). Similarly, an American in a UK chemist asking for rubbers will be redirected to the stationery store where he might meet the Aussie on his way to the chemist.

Q: MANY GUIDE BOOKS DESCRIBE THE BRITS AS VERY POLITE.

A: This stems from the fact that the Brits generally — the southern English in particular — use the words please and thank you a great deal. The Scots use these terms far less, not because they are less polite than their neighbours, but simply because the Scots find their frequent use unnecessarily ingratiating and superfluous in most exchanges. A pub exchange in Surrey might run:

A gin and tonic, please.
Right sir, a gin and tonic, thank you sir. There you go sir, thank you.
How much is that please?
Two pounds fifty please sir.
There we are, thank you.
Thank you sir.
Your change sir, thank you very much.
Oh, thank you.

In Scotland or the US the exchange would be just as amiable but shorn of all the repetitive niceties.

In Spain, despite the English phrase books inclusion of **por favor** and **gracias** at the end of almost every sentence, hardly anyone uses please and thank you. In Ireland, they tend to use the conditional tense or just the barman's name. **A pint of Guinness, Michael**, or, **Would you give me a pint of Guinness and a gin and tonic?** English husbands and wives can sound amazingly lacking in intimacy: 'May I have the butter please darling'. It is the recurrence of the polite terms which convinces the casual observer that the people are so mannerly. There is also a fashion which began a couple of decades back for mothers and fathers to add please to parental instructions, producing the incongruous, 'Stop doing that Wayne, please!', 'Tracey, come here this minute please!' or 'Sharon, please get down from there this instant!'

In this context, watch the English TV game show Countdown. The object of the game is to make words out of random letters. The contestant has to ask the hostess for a series of letters and they invariably say, 'A consonant please Carol. And a vowel please Carol.' The hostess, Carol Vorderman, regularly replies to the requests with, 'Thank you'.

All very strange to non-Southern ears.

Q: Isn't that a good thing?

A: It would be if it was more than the simple acquisition of words. Good manners are all about graciousness, charm, warmth and making people feel at ease. In other countries, many exchanges are a delight of courtesy and grace without the need for any pat phrases. Amongst friends in a continental bar it would be considered too formal and distant to use 'thank you'. The absence of such formal politeness is a mark of friendship and intimacy.

Q: What have the Brits got against bus shelters?

A: Like trainspotting and fluffy dice this is another mystery. We've seen four-sided shelters, three-sided, two-sided and single-sided with a roof in the shape of a figure seven. They've had metal sides, laminated glass sides and clear reinforced plastic sides. They've been painted primary colours and soothing pastel shades. Some had flat roofs, others convex roofs. No matter what, for some inexplicable reason, within days of erection, a whole pane of plastic will lie shattered on the ground like the contents of so many ice buckets. If the sides are still intact they are covered in either painted on or carved on graffiti. Some are so badly scarred that when the sun catches the plastic, the entire once see-through side becomes opaque.

Shelters have been fitted with fixed bucket-seats, fold-down seats, swivel seats and mesh seats — most have been vandalised. The latest introduction is the rigid angled bar with a width of some four inches. You can't take the weight off your feet but you can rest your buttocks (well, four inches of them) on the bar.

But why bus shelters? No-one knows. Phone boxes tend to be left intact, street signs, belisha beacons and advertising hoardings seem to cause no offence, but the poor innocuous bus shelter somehow attracts a violent reaction wholly disproportionate to its passive and protective nature. Perhaps it's shelter rage.

Q: You also seem to have a problem with your public lavatories?

A: The biggest problem with these is the extreme differences in standards and accessibility. For example, the public loos opposite Glasgow Cathedral don't open till 11am. Most coach tours pick up around 8am so a coach party from Edinburgh would arrive in Glasgow an hour later, with possibly 50 people looking for a loo.They are the responsibility of the local council. East Lothian Council employs attendants in the public loos and some of these facilities have received world-wide acclaim for their cleanliness. Some attendants vie with others for the best standards, bringing in fresh flowers and hanging pictures on their spotless walls. Visitors have even been known to visit the public loos in towns like Haddington and North Berwick just to admire them.

Fife Council charge 10p for a pee but it is worth it as they too are of a high standard. It does seem a tad strange at St Andrews though, where the attendant opposite the hallowed Old Course is collecting 10p coins from wealthy visitors who spend about £100 for a round of golf. One exception is Culross in Fife, a delightful and beautifully preserved historic town where the public loo is so evil as to merit a wad of Semtex.

Q: WHY ARE YOUR STREETS ALWAYS SO LITTERED?

A: They are bad aren't they? There has always been a tendency to throw sweet wrappers, cigarette packets and other small debris on the street, but things have actually worsened. You see people throwing polystyrene food containers on the street as well as empty Coke and Irn-Bru tins, and it's not just kids either, you'll see parents do it in front of their kids. The streets of Glasgow and Edinburgh are also peppered with discarded chewing gum.

But why?

One reason is that the problem is self-perpetuating. They would not do it in Switzerland simply because nobody, but nobody, does it in any of the 26 Swiss Cantons. But, seeing so many others do it in Britain encourages yet more. Young people may think it is rebellious and anti-Establishment and that litter bins are for wimps. A lot of the blame can be laid on the creation of the great tower block housing schemes which burgeoned from the mid-20th century. Most of the people housed there were poor, often unemployed and with low aspirations. The schemes were without heart, with none of the old friendly shops, no public parks, few amenities and probably no pub or restaurant. Billy Connolly coined the memorable phrase 'deserts with windaes.' Any pub tended to be on the rough side where the courtesies of the genial 'mine host' were unknown.

Such an environment can induce feelings of being an outsider, worthlessness and even despair. What money there was would be spent on some form of escape — gambling, cigarettes, drink, drugs or an endless diet of TV not unlike that depicted in Trainspotting. Some of the schemes produce unemployment figures in excess of three times the national average. A recent report from the Child Poverty Action Group revealed that between a quarter and a third of Scottish Children were living in poverty conditions. So putting food containers, drinks tins or cigarette packets neatly in a bin or picking up dog excrement is not a priority for many. The anti-social behaviour in the poorer areas is carried on to the city streets.

Q: SO IT'S A STATE OF MIND?

A: Largely; take Glasgow with its set of special problems. The post-war rebuilding of the economy peaked in the 1960s when the then Prime Minister, Harold MacMillan, declared that Britain had 'never had it so good'. An economic plateau ensued followed by a steady downturn. With massive lay-offs from the huge industrial base – shipbuilding, coal, steel, motor manufacture and the tobacco industries – unemployment hit hard. The shipyards alone once employed in excess of 100,000 people. Roughly one person in ten was dependent on a wage from the yards. This excludes all the ancillary industries such as furniture for ships, piping, electric fittings and the innumerable links in the supply chain. Add some 30,000 mining jobs from Lanarkshire and contiguous areas, the unemployed from Ravenscraig steel works, the motor manufacturing jobs at Linwood and Bathgate, the textile industry in Paisley which in turn wiped out so many pubs, cafes, newsagents etc, and the picture became even grimmer.

To service the city, Glasgow had to increase its local taxes and some of the middle classes moved out to the leafy suburbs and into other boroughs. Glasgow City was then faced with fewer payers and a proportionately higher number of low paid and unemployed people. Less money meant fewer services, fewer street cleaners, fewer litter bins and a bigger litter problem which as we know adds to the self perpetuation of the problem. Glasgow is now forced to apply high Council Tax rates with fewer public services. Using some hard figures to illustrate — a band 'D' home (value: £225,000) in London's seriously wealthy Kensington pays £698 in local Council Tax. A band 'D' home in Glasgow (value: £95,000) pays £1154. In cash ratios that's 322:1 and 82:1.

Needless to say, this is not a national or regional problem, it is a social one and can be witnessed in Chicago, Liverpool, Detroit or any of the so-called inner city areas where the more affluent have moved to the periphery. Despite the deprivation angle, the British as a whole, and Scots in particular, are very careless with litter. Even great tourist attractions and beauty spots can be defiled. Balloch for example, on the bonnie, bonnie banks of Loch Lomond can be so litter-strewn as to be an embarrassment.

One other factor is size. Dundee for example, has had similar problems with poverty yet it is small enough for the people to feel a sense of ownership so the litter problem is nowhere near as bad as in the larger conurbations.

Q: WHY DO YOU DRIVE ON THE WRONG SIDE OF THE ROAD?

A: The practice is said to originate from the days when the horse was the primary means of transport. By keeping to the left hand side, a rider could reach for his sword in self defence and brandish it on the 'off' side. *But we don't see too many horsemen on the roads and none seem to have swords!* True, but it has a great deal to do with being an island — habits, practices and thinking become insular. *Will the UK ever change sides?* In the days of 'A' and 'B' roads it would have been possible to switch sides but now, with the motorway system and thousands of graduated filter lanes angled in the 'wrong' direction, it would be too daunting a task to undertake. Planning road networks such as the M8/M74 interchange on the eastern edge of Glasgow must have been a nightmare; to re-plan them where every route is reversed would just not be practical.

Why not at least have your road signs in kilometres?

No reason. The Irish still drive on the left hand side but all their road signs are in kilometres, although for a period, driving in Ireland could be disconcerting. The distance signs were changed on a piecemeal basis, just a few at a time. When driving from say, Dublin to Belfast, it was common to see 'Belfast 60' on a distance sign then 'Belfast 80' on the next sign, the latter having been converted to kilometres. Now the mile, like the Irish Punt, is history.

Q: THE SCOTTISH ROAD NETWORK IS QUITE POOR.

A: For a small country of five million people our roads are not bad but, by European standards, they are poor. An Automobile Association report in Feb 2002 disclosed that of the ten most dangerous roads in Britain, eight were in the Highlands of Scotland. The fact which rankles most with Scotland is that you can drive on motorways from Exeter on the English Channel to Carlisle yet from Carlisle to Scotland's largest city there is still no continuous motorway. Worse, on one of the oldest highways in the land, from the English capital, London, to the Scottish capital, Edinburgh, there are still long stretches of single carriageway hardly worthy of B-road status. Ironically, the very name of the road suggests something of a superlative, the A1. Even more surprisingly, 50 years after the first motorway (the M1) began, there is still no continuous motorway between Edinburgh and Glasgow.

Q: ANY SCOTTISH ENTERTAINMENTS I SHOULD GO TO?

A: Entertainment is very much the same the world over, eating, drinking, cinema, theatre and discos. However, one Scottish entertainment experience worth a visit is the bars that specialise in Scottish folk music or more broadly, the Celtic connection with music from Ireland, Scotland, Brittany and Nova Scotia.

Q: WHERE CAN I BUY SEX?

A: Just about every town in the world will have its own 'red light' area. In Scotland there are escort agencies, sauna and massage parlours and lap-dancing clubs. Prostitution by telephone is also common, not unlike ordering a pizza. If you want some titillation and no more, there are some pubs around with performing strippers (still called Go-go dancing by some). If you can derive some scintilla of pleasure from a woman talking dirty to you over the phone, there is a seemingly endless choice of numbers to choose from in that backbone of British journalism, the red-topped tabloid press, as well as in magazines of an anatomic and glossy disposition.

Certainly aural or visual titillation is the safest choice. Edinburgh provides around twenty sauna and massage establishments where sex menus include the incredibly coy hand relief, oral (as opposed to aural) or the full Monty. If you are turned on by the risk of kerb crawling or strolling through the red-light areas, then the Blythswood area in Glasgow is the place and Leith in Edinburgh. Aberdeen and Dundee have their own areas but they change every so often as the police, in an exercise in utter futility, move the girls on. Glasgow has a higher ratio of street-walkers because of the 'Catholic-Calvinist' alliance. Saunas find it much harder to obtain licences from the God-fearing council, so the girls have to sell sex on the streets with all the concomitant risks of violence, theft, rape and, on occasion, murder. Male 'escort services' are now much more in evidence and discussing such a service no longer carries the taboo of yesteryear.

Q: HOW CAN I BE SURE IF THE WOMAN IS A PROSTITUTE?

A: If you need to ask a question like that it might be wiser to stick to the top shelf do-it-yourself magazines. However, should you make a mistake of that nature, the clatter round the ear you will receive from a worthy Scottish wifie will leave you in no doubt whatever as to the nature of your error.

Q: WHAT IS THE GAY SCENE LIKE?

A: Britain as a whole has had great conflicts about homosexuality. In March 2003 a member of the government, Ron Davies, was forced to resign after it was revealed he had had a sexual encounter with another man in a Somerset picnic area. Had it been with a woman, not a flicker of interest would have been shown. The fact that he felt it necessary to lie about the incident is a reflection of the intolerance of our society. Worse, a cameraman from one of our tabloid newspapers lay in wait for Mr Davies, which says as much about its readership as it does about the paper itself. While the Far East, Middle East and most of Europe has had a very laissez faire attitude towards the issue, the Brits have always had great difficulty with the subject. In a country where 'bugger' and 'sod' are terms of endearment, debates on the acceptability of homosexual practices seem to evoke great passions along with waves of disapproval in the right-wing press.

Historically, the Church of England has always had a disproportionately high number of gay priests. It tended to attract the more aesthetic and non-macho sons of the middle and upper classes. Yet the Anglican church hierarchy has consistently condemned the ordaining of gay priests, though fully cognisant of the sexual orientation of a substantial minority. The Conservatives have always been the most intolerant, though ironically, many Tories had been to all-male private boarding schools where the only sexual experience boys acquired was with other boys. Perhaps the Tory hostility was borne of a sense of self-consciousness or shame.

Scotland has always had more problems about coming out. The macho culture bred from hard physical work whether on the land, on trawlers, in coalmines, shipbuilding, steelworks or in any of the hard manual trades, consigned any form of softness to a back seat. The climate alone is a permanent challenge to demonstrative affection of any kind. Add to this a rather joyless form of Calvinism and the Catholic disappoval of any form of sexual pleasure and the scene is not set for a carnival of erotic abandon. Scottish men have always had difficulty in expressing their deepest emotions, even to their womenfolk, so coming to terms with gay love has not been easy.

Q: WON'T THE PERCENTAGE OF GAY BRITS BE THE SAME AS ANYWHERE ELSE?

A: Of course. Despite the French allusion to *le vice Anglais*, sexual propensity will be universal, it is only attitudes and levels of hypocrisy or double standards which change.

The British parliament has agonised over the legalisation of homosexuality, then the age of consent, then the acceptability of acknowledging it in the school curriculum, the depiction of it on TV or film and whether gay couples could adopt children.

Despite the legality of a gay lifestyle, politicians and others in the public eye may still be nervous about coming out.

Q: HAS THE DUST SETTLED NOW?

A: Pretty much so. Most British cities now have a busy gay scene with gay clubs and bars. The media now reflects more accurately the gay section of society. Derogatory terms such as queer or nancy boy have all but disappeared. Many TV stars and game show hosts are not only gay but quite demonstratively so and seem to be all the more popular because of it. Many prominent people have 'come out' and the general feeling is to wonder what all the fuss was about it the first place. There are still some old dyed-in-the-wool hard-liners and sadly the odd report of 'gay bashing' but Britain is catching up with the rest of the world. Ironically it was holy Catholic conservative Ireland which introduced more liberal legislation before swinging Britain.

Q: WHAT'S WITH THE BRITISH TABLOID'S OBSESSION WITH BREASTS?

A: Yes it is an embarrassment. There is something quite puerile in the endless repetition of topless women on the front pages of what are now known as the red-topped tabloids. One of these exponents of skid-row journalism actually went so far as to boast a 'nipple count' on the front page indicating just how many breasts were to be seen inside. Not that they call them breasts, they usually opt for the juvenile terms knockers or boobs. Some of the red-top tabloids actually print the word 'censored' just over the nipples which is another British mystery comparable to trainspotting and fluffy-dice. It is a behaviour pattern similar to that of schoolboys of a generation ago who could be found sniggering over some naughty drawing or photograph and delighting in their new-found knowledge of worldly things.

Red-top cameramen cannot resist photographing a woman leaving a car and showing her knickers – peeping-tom behaviour at its most base. Most of the language of the tabloids is of an infantile nature: people don't have sexual intercourse, they 'bonk'; sexual liaisons are never delightful, they are invariably 'sordid'; intercourse other than once a night in the privacy of the bed is bound to be 'kinky sex' or 'a five times a night romp'; no heading can be without such witty alliteration as 'Babs bares her boobs in bonking beano'; a prostitute is usually a 'sordid vice girl'; a politician, or better still a vicar, found leaving a brothel, is sure to be described as 'sleazy'.

Q: Isn't it all quite old fashioned?

A: Very much so but it is probably the level of hypocrisy that is most offensive. The red-tops share a limited vocabulary of descriptions which exude disapproval — 'sleazy vice-girl in bonking romp with kinky bishop' conveys a tone of critical disgust more typical of the famous Clean Up TV campaigner Mary Whitehouse. Yet these papers owe their very existence to selling sex whether through their 'nipple count' or through the adverts they carry for a wide range of eroticism.

Who's Mary Whitehouse?

Was. She founded the Clean Up TV Campaign in 1964. Although well-intentioned she frequently shot herself in the foot by referring to any televised eroticism as 'dirty', 'filthy' or 'disgusting'. But you're right, it is very old fashioned. It all began with international newspaper proprietor Rupert Murdoch. He bought over a UK paper called the *Sun* that at the time (1960s) was a middle-of-the-road broadsheet. Allegedly, Murdoch was reported as saying, 'We need more tit in the *Sun*'. The remaining journalists argued with him saying Britain was now more mature, that people needed better information and better presentation. Murdoch insisted on his tits theory and to the nation's shame, he was proved correct. Within a year the *Sun* was a serious rival to the massive sales of the *Daily Mirror* and shortly after was outselling it.

Alas, the situation continues; while it might be assumed that grown-up men (and it is mainly men) would tire of a daily dose of Mickey Mouse journalism and mammary madness, it has not been the case; the red-tops continue to sell in large numbers. One defence from the red-top buyers is that the sports coverage is good. There may be truth in this but many might respond with the old Scots term, 'Aye, that'll be right'. The sports pages justification is reminiscent of the *Playboy* buyer who insisted he bought it for the quality of the articles it contained.

Q: Maybe the working man likes the *Sun* for its political leaning?

A: It doesn't appear so. Historically the main tabloids – the *Daily Mirror* and the *Daily Record* – were supporters of the Labour Party as were their readers. Murdoch and his *Sun* not only enticed away the other tabloid's readers with his combination of wink-

wink-nudge-nudge articles and exposed flesh but he even changed the political bias of the paper from left to right and still the readers continued to buy his paper. The *Sun* went so far as to boast of political muscle with the notorious headline, 'It was the *Sun* that won it', after a Conservative general election victory which the paper had heavily backed. Even this provocative headline failed to alienate the solidly working-class Labour voter.

So the British would rather have breasts than balanced journalism?
Sadly, it is hard to reach any other conclusion. It appears to be a peculiarly British eccentricity. Continental countries such as France and Spain do a good trade in comics, often pornographic ones, but tend to leave their newspapers for news. Only in Britain is there a sort of amalgam of soft porn magazine, comic book and newspaper. The red-top writers fall over themselves to use the most childish and predictable comic-book puns. No exposed bottom can avoid such brilliant journalese as 'it's a bum wrap' or the inevitable use of the word cheeky.

Ex-cabinet minister, Clare Short, once denounced the *Sun* for its 'page three' culture. When she resigned over the Iraqi war some years later, the *Sun* couldn't restrain its delight. Completely bypassing the political significance, it told its readers what a dreadful old frumpish kill-joy Clare was.

Q: WHAT DO SCOTTISH WOMEN THINK?

A: Scottish writer Hannah McGill writing in the *Sunday Herald* in January 2003 expressed her disgust that the *Sun* had appointed its first female editor, Rebekah Wade, who made it plain she had no plans to change Murdoch's tits formula.

Maybe she sees it as harmless fun?
Hannah McGill and most intelligent women deeply resent that argument. They respond that the powerful forces of profit have brainwashed people into the fear of appearing narrow-minded or prudish by objecting to naked women in a so-called newspaper. They believe that children brought up in a *Sun* reader's home will believe, to quote Hannah McGill, that the function of young women's gender 'is to provide light entertainment'. She added that 'Page three girls are to women what golliwogs and the Black and White Minstrels are to black people — grinning puppets that exist to remind us all that we're still subjugated, still trivialised, still figures of fun.'

Strong stuff!
Very much so. But if such a powerful feeling of resentment exists, you can see just how infuriating the tabloids must be to the thinking woman and – lest it be overlooked – thinking man.

Q: WOULD YOU RECOMMEND A BURNS SUPPER FOR MY WIFE AND ME?

A: Ten years ago one would have hesitated to answer. This was a bit of a hot potato. A Burns Supper is a wonderful experience. It contains many riches, poetry, song, patriotism, nostalgia, raw emotion, humour, love and brotherhood. It's the last quality which used to be the problem. Most Burns Suppers were once all-male affairs. Regularly there were letters in the Scottish press from visitors of Scots descent expressing their disgust at being unable to attend a Burns Night as man and wife. Alas, the drinking fraternity in Scotland had traditionally been just that, a fraternity. Fortunately the all-male ramparts have been breached at Burns Suppers and in most situations.

Many pubs were once men-only shops or if women were allowed they might be consigned to the snug. However, as golf clubs are beginning to lose their misogynist habits, most Burns Supper nights have abandoned their all-male status.

Check in advance but if you have the opportunity to attend, do. There may be many lines of Burns which are indecipherable to the non-Scots ear but you can read up the more popular of Burns' works beforehand, such as *Holy Wullie's Prayer*, *Tam O'Shanter* or *Ode to a Mouse*. Don't hesitate to ask a native Scot to translate the Scots words you don't understand. It may be you'll catch out your proud native Scot.

Q: WHY WERE BURNS SUPPERS ALL-MALE PRESERVES?

A: Scottish migrants took many of their traditions with them — Highland Games, Pipe Bands, Burns Suppers, Auld Lang Syne at New Year and, of course, the water of life. The New World produces its own brand of the events though. Scotland tended to keep the sexist attitude because Burns and many of his fans enjoyed the brotherhood of man and Freemasonry. Drinking was very much a male pursuit and Freemasonry was an exclusively male club. Less rigid fans of the supper ritual can find *The Toast to The Lassies* a bit too patronising for their taste. *What happens there?* Women were invariably employed to wait on the male diners, providing their haggis, neeps and tatties followed by coffee and shortbread but, once the women had fulfilled their function, a toast was offered to them. This sounds quite gracious but many saw it as a dismissal heralding the purely male business of some serious drinking to accompany the music, recitation and frequently off-colour speeches.

Q: SO MIXED BURNS SUPPERS ARE THE NORM NOW?

A: Yes indeed. But there may still exist an example of female resentment regarding the past. The following 'response from the lassies' was given by the author's wife Bernice at a Burns Supper in 2003:

> A reply from the lassies was quite a nice thought
> From men who considered us so easily bought
> The historic Burns Supper was an all male affair
> With female guest-speakers disappointingly rare.
> The few women involved could serve up the grub
> But when all was consumed, came the inevitable snub
> ***The toast to the lassies*** was the signal to go
> Leaving alcohol and testosterone to liberally flow
> So when the emotions and the cups had run dry
> And Burns' compassion had made grown men cry
> Back to the kitchen went the haggis-smeared knives
> Back home went the menfolk to long-suffering wives
> But now boys, thank God, the times are a-changing
> And political correctness is extremely wide-ranging
> So let's toast not the lassies nor the laddies so braw
> Let's get pissed together — here's tae one and tae a'

The Bard of Dunbar 2003

Q: THE BRITS SEEM TO DRINK A LOT.

A: Yes. The Scots, the Irish, the northern English and the Welsh do drink much more than, say, the Americans. There are many reasons, such as religious disapproval, the climate, the licensing laws, the buy-your-round ethos, macho imagery in the adverts, male bonding, poverty of aspiration and more. As with Burns Suppers, the macho association with drink has dwindled and now young women can be just as drunk and disorderly as their bibulous brothers.

While kids in mainland Europe are brought up in a café society where alcohol is part of everyday life, British kids were excluded from licensed premises. As with smoking, taking a drink seemed adult, manly, sophisticated and cool.

Scotland used to be much, much worse. Prior to 1976 the pubs shut at 10pm and stayed shut on Sundays. It was quite common for men to drink more than they could handle or enjoy, in the ten or fifteen minutes leading up to the 10pm curfew. Many pubs would commence lining up rows of glasses of whisky in expectation of the 'last orders' panic. Scenes of men staggering along the pavements or vomiting in the streets were common.

Q: OTHER COUNTRIES AND SOME AMERICAN STATES HAVE BEEN AS STRICT.

A: Sure. The US 'bible belt' states can be pretty bleak as can parts of Scandinavia. Russia has a big problem, particularly in winter when drunks can be found frozen to death. We Brits exported the curfew concept to places like Australia where they were forced to endure 'the six o'clock swill' as pubs shut their doors at the unbelievably early time of 6pm. Those leaving their work at five had one hour to consume amazing amounts of beer before the bell. Glasses used to be lined up on the bar and filled by a hose.

Though the Calvinistas fought against liberalising the laws, they eventually had to agree that the Scottish drinking scene is infinitely more civilised than before the dark days of 1976. Today's young people seldom go out much before the once dreaded 10 o' clock. Australians ditched the British influenced laws many years ago and adopted attitudes towards licensing more consistent with those of their mainland European immigrants.

Surprisingly, in England where heavy drinking was less of a problem, the licensing laws are much more repressive than in Scotland. An interesting paradox is that the English holiday-maker in Spain will expect to drink all night and disco till dawn, yet back home he will obediently drink up and exit the pub at 11pm.

Q: WHO ARE YOUR FAVOURITE TOURISTS?

A: Tricky one this as one never wishes to offend a guest. However, most people in the industry would nominate the Americans as favourite visitors. There is a solid reason for this. Less than 10% of the US population hold passports. Logically, why should they? When your national boundaries include Alaska and Hawaii, The Rockies, The Pacific, the Atlantic and the Gulf of Mexico and span half a dozen time zones, who needs a passport? Those citizens who have them tend to be the better educated, the wealthier, the more courteous and the more interested in other cultures.

Also, because of the egalitarian nature of American society, they are generally friendly to all they meet. They can be quite gregarious (by British standards) and open. They lack shyness and inhibition and consequently ask questions that might appear dumb to some. On history they can confuse kings and queens and be centuries out in their dates, but they don't care. They are happy to ask and be corrected.

They are also generous tippers, no?

Well yes, tipping is the norm in the US and is also probably more generous than we are used to. But to attribute the popularity of the Americans solely to a mercenary motive would not be true.

What about the downside?

All drivers and guides like a happy bus with passengers laughing, chatting and interacting. Some northern Europeans and Scandinavians can be a little quiet which – though they can be perfectly happy – can make us nervous. The Japanese, Taiwanese and Koreans are invariably courteous and seldom complain. The Irish, now coming to Scotland in much greater numbers, are consistently good humoured and easy-going. The southern Europeans are friendly and expressive. Alas, some of our 'lunch stops' leave them noticeably underwhelmed. The southern English can appear a little inhibited and can be heard to whisper to one another asides such as, 'No, you ask him'.

CHAPTER 4
RELIGION

Q: HOW COME THERE ARE SO MANY CHURCHES IN SCOTLAND?

A: Throughout the UK churches have always had a prominent position – often quite literally – on high ground, hence the origin of the steeplechase. Edinburgh for example is awash with church buildings. The city boasts three cathedrals, the historic St Giles, the seat of Presbyterianism on the High St, the magnificent St Mary's Episcopalian Cathedral in the West End and the 19th-century St Mary's Roman Catholic Cathedral to the east at the top of Leith Walk. In Broughton St to the north of the RC cathedral, in just a half-mile, can be found eight buildings designed as places of worship.

Are they used? For all sorts of purposes, but worshippers are thin on the ground these days. Some buildings have been converted into living accommodation, some have been given over to mammon for the sale of goods and not a few have been converted into function halls that are venues for any number of theatrical productions during the Edinburgh Festival. One of Edinburgh's popular clubs, Café Graffiti, was located downstairs in Mansfield Place Church on Broughton St. The painter John Bellamy spoke of his boyhood in the village of Port Seton on the Firth of Forth with no fewer than 12 churches. Now, the mainly elderly worshippers would fit comfortably into one.

Moffat, the market town in northern Dumfriesshire was a popular spa town in Victorian times. Many well-to-do people built villas there for the summer season and the town was obliged to have places of worship large enough to seat the entire population. The result is that this fairly average-sized town is blessed with massive churches, one of which, St Andrews, is still the largest parish church in South-west Scotland with seating for 1,150 people.

Q: WHAT'S THE DIFFERENCE BETWEEN THE CHURCH OF SCOTLAND, THE CHURCH OF ENGLAND, THE CHURCH OF IRELAND AND THE CHURCH OF WALES?

A: Take the last one first ... it's the church in Wales. The church in Wales is the Anglican Church (Church of England). The Anglicans stopped short of using the term The Church of Wales because the predominant faiths in Wales were of the Low Church variety, mainly Methodist and Baptist, so the term The Church of Wales might have seemed a bit presumptuous, even arrogant. However, no such sensitivities were shown to the Irish. Although the Irish clung to the old Roman Catholic religion, the newly reformed religion was formally named The Church of Ireland. Here the plot thickens because The Church of Scotland is indeed the church of Scotland, the Presbyterian Church. The difference being that the title was agreed at the Act of Union in 1707 by (ostensibly) equal partners, whereas Ireland was treated as a British colony or possession and was told what was what, rather than conferred with.

Q: SO WHY DID ENGLAND AND SCOTLAND CHOOSE DIFFERENT RELIGIONS?

A: Make yourself comfortable and pour yourself a good measure of the golden fluid. What the Big Bang was to astronomers, the Reformation was to Christians. The medieval church had grown so corrupt that reform was inevitable. Martin Luther's public protest was the first recorded, in 1517 (when John Knox of Scotland was only five years old and John Calvin of Geneva eight). A general cynicism towards the church prevailed but there was little spontaneous demand for change.

The catalyst in England was Henry VIII's need for an annulment of his first marriage to Catherine of Aragon. The pope wouldn't play ball, not entirely motivated by the sanctity of Christian marriage but also because Catherine's nephew was Emperor Charles V who ruled the European roost and all sovereigns answered to him. But Thomas Cromwell, Henry's first minister, had a cunning plan. He passed the Restraint of Appeals Act in 1533, which in essence forbade any breach of national sovereignty such as an appeal to any outside power, ergo it was none of the pope's business what Henry did. This was followed in 1534 by the Act of Supremacy which gave supremacy of the church to the crown. Game set and match to Hal.

Q: AND SCOTLAND WAS AN INDEPENDENT COUNTRY WITH ITS OWN MONARCH?

A: Precisely, the main difference between Scotland and England was that the Henrician (Henry's) Reformation was legal and jurisdictional, whereas Scotland was influenced more by the doctrinal issues. The dissolution of the monasteries didn't bother the people much as they were viewed more as land-owning corporations rather than centres of spiritual retreat. In 1563, the 39 Articles that codified the Anglican faith established the Church of England very much as it remains today. Because Henry's motivation for change was personal rather than spiritual, the church remained, to a large degree, structurally intact. The Church of England retained archbishops, bishops, canons etc leaving the hierarchical format relatively unchanged. Also, there was no great doctrinal rejection of incense, church music and hymns, ornate vestments, stained glass and all the gothic splendour associated with High Church worship.

In Scotland the motives were more pure. Patrick Hamilton from St Andrews heard Calvin preach in Geneva and when he returned to Scotland he was so fired up with Calvinistic zeal that he began to spread the word. Alas, the fat cats of the old church didn't take too kindly to this young whippersnapper advocating reform and poor Pat was put to death. You can see the very spot in St Andrews where his initials are formed in cobbles on North Street. There is also an obelisk hard by the Old Course commemorating the other four Protestant martyrs who suffered a similar fate.

The man behind such fearful retribution was David Beaton who was made a Cardinal in 1538 and in the following year succeeded his uncle as Archbishop of St Andrews. Beaton was the effective ruler of Scotland during the regency of Arran.

Q: ARRAN?

A: When Mary became Queen of Scots in 1542 she was only six days old, so somebody had to mind the store until she was old enough to look after it herself. After Mary of Guise (mother of the queen) was overthrown by the Lords of the Congregation, the Earl of Arran, James Hamilton, was given the job. Hamilton and Beaton were the top dogs of the period.

Martyring the first lot of Protestants didn't go down well with the people and, after the death of George Wishart, the good folk of St Andrews broke into Beaton's splendid palace and put him to death. Not satisfied with that, they torched the magnificent St Andrews Cathedral. Its remaining gable ends and quite remarkable dimensions stand today to give testament as to how great a feat of architecture it was.

The Reformation in Scotland took longer to settle. There was friction between the Congregational (anti-hierarchy) and Episcopalian (pro-hierarchy) wings of the new Kirk. Episcopacy (having bishops) was abolished in 1638 after some uncertainty because of the Catholic Jacobite monarchy. The 1688 Glorious Revolution settled the matter in favour of a fully Presbyterian system of church government. But even then there were rifts and splits. In 1747 there were the anti-burghers or members of The Scottish Secession Church, then there was The Disruption of 1843 producing The Free Church of Scotland followed by the United Free Church of Scotland and the Free Presbyterian Church.

Q: AND EACH NEW SPLIT REQUIRED NEW CHURCHES?

A: Quite. Of course, along with the Presbyterian sub-divisions, the Catholics are still in business, particularly in Glasgow and the west coast due to Irish immigration and an influx of Catholic Highlanders to the industrialised central belt. Then there's the Episcopalian/Anglican/Church of England wing plus all the other Christian denominations such as Methodist, Baptist, Unitarians, Seventh Day Adventists, Quakers, right down to individual clerics who formed their own breakaway churches such as the late Pastor Jack Glass in Scotland and Ian Paisley in Northern Ireland. Of course, there are also the synagogues, mosques and temples of other faiths.

Q: IT MUST BE CONFUSING HAVING SO MANY DENOMINATIONS?

A: From a global perspective all religions have their splits and schisms. Muslims and Jews have several sects, each one claiming to be purer than the other. The US has so many Christian sects as to make the mind boggle. Universally there seems to be a normative scale from Fundamentalist to Liberal and all religions (and political parties for that matter) produce factions that place themselves somewhere along that line. Even the Catholics, who claim unity as a big factor in their faith, were riven by disagreements on birth control, purgatory and the Latin Mass.

Q: BUT SCOTLAND IS SUCH A SMALL COUNTRY, WHY SO MANY SPLITS?

A: In fairness, all the fundamentalists were decent God-fearing people who believed salvation lay in the purest and simplest interpretation of the bible. The only trouble was that in their zeal for reform, some of them might, just might, have thrown the baby out with the bath water. Also, the more fundamentalist wings have received a very bad press.

Q: WHY A BAD PRESS?

A: Take for example Sabbath Day observance. The Good Book is pretty laid back about this saying simply, keep the day holy. It is the fundamentalist interpretation of 'holy' that has attracted such scorn. Not hanging out washing on a Sunday, not listening to the radio (other than perhaps suitable programmes) and a whole raft of disapproving censures, most notable in the Western

Highlands and Islands where the fundamentalists were strongest. The more liberal press delighted in poking fun at no alcohol sales on Sunday, no ferries, no amusements ... even children's swings were known to be chained up lest some enjoyment might be derived from them on the Sabbath. All things High Church (aka papist) were rejected leading to an ignoring of saints' days and the liturgical calendar where even Christmas Day was treated as an ordinary working day, not just in the fundamentalist belt but throughout Scotland. Schools in the Outer Hebrides were denied Christmas trees — quite illogically, as the Christmas tree has no religious significance whatever. In some quarters the very use of Christian names was considered a trifle 'High' and a fashion grew in the use of surnames as first names as in Cameron, Crawford or Farquhar.

Q: SURELY THIS IS ALL HISTORY NOW?

A: Much of it is — mainly through the forces of commercialism and the ubiquitous TV. Scottish houses which at one time would not have displayed a flickering candle are now ablaze with coloured lights reminiscent of the strip in Las Vegas. Christmas Day is a holiday, as is Boxing Day and so is the entire week between Christmas and New Year for many.

Q: YOU SAY 'MUCH OF IT' — DO YOU STILL HAVE FUNDAMENTALIST AREAS?

A: Some, much to the delight of the 'progressive' tabloid press. Not long ago the Minister for the Highlands and Islands and Gaelic, Alasdair Morrison MSP, formally opened the annual festival of Gaelic music and dance known by the Gaelic word Mod. His official function on the island of Harris seems innocuous enough but his church, the Free Presbyterian Church, condemned Mr Morrison and went so far as to refuse to baptise his children. **Why?**

Well, the Mod – being a festival of music, dance and literature – has a long association with cavorting, having fun and the liberal consumption of strong drink, so much so that the Mod is also known as the Whisky Olympics. So by association, Mr Morrison was deemed an unfit person to care for the moral welfare of his children.

Q: BUT WHAT ABOUT BASIC CHRISTIAN CHARITY?

A: No need to ask. The correspondence columns of the Scottish papers were full of outrage by Christians and non-Christians alike on the subject of Christian love and tolerance (or intolerance as the case may be). It even triggered internecine disputes within the Christian family.

But wouldn't this be a one-off by a single church minister?

Would that it were. Alas, only a few years previously, the most senior judge in the land, Lord MacKay of Clashfern was condemned by the same church for attending the funeral and requiem mass of a Catholic colleague. There are other instances as well. For example, the Free Presbyterian Church in Northern Ireland has condemned line dancing as immoral. *Line dancing?* Yes, no need to say, it sounds more like Catholic fundamentalism. We all know that dancing can be a vertical expression of a horizontal intention but with line dancing you are on your own, you don't even touch anyone.

However, Northern Ireland fundamentalists are not over blessed with a sense of humour. When the law decriminalising homosexuality was introduced in Northern Ireland, Ian Paisley was on the streets with placards reading 'Save Northern Ireland from Buggery' as if the land was on the threshold of a ferment of gay debauchery. When the licensing laws were to be liberalised, the same cleric told the BBC, 'Let them drink the Lord's good water' which conveyed just a suggestion of a lack of understanding of the desire for a glass or two of the grape or grain. Worse, fundamentalist posters can be seen in parts of 'Orange' country reading 'Alcohol is the Devil's vomit'. Still, what it lacks in subtlety it makes up for in clarity.

Q: WERE THERE NO CATHOLIC FUNDAMENTALISTS?

A: Plenty. One of the reasons Scotland could be such a dour place was because where the Calvinists failed to condemn something you could guarantee the Roman Catholics would stamp on it. *Such as?* The Calvinists came down hard on drink, card playing and dancing in general but specifically dances that went beyond midnight on a Saturday and thus offended God by continuing into the Sabbath. They disapproved of frivolities, gaiety and any form of merry-making. The Catholic Church developed a terror of the only remaining pleasure — sex. Some say that a celibate clergy having been denied any pleasures of the flesh were going to make damn sure nobody else had a good time. Certainly where Catholicism dominated as it did in Ireland – particularly during the reign of Archbishop John Charles McQuaid – sex was all but removed from the dictionaries. Impure acts merited hellfire but, as nobody 'did it' (apart from solitary sex), 'impure thoughts' were just as bad, as were 'occasions of sin'. Catholic boys were cautioned against staying in the bath too long. Many of these innocents thought it was a caution against sloth. There was the famous 'index' of books where the works of writers could be listed as not being suitable for pure Catholic minds. Paradoxically, included on this list was Graham Greene's *The Quiet American*. Greene was a Catholic convert whose deep theological reflections ran through all his works. Nevertheless, one of England's great literary giants was consigned to Room 101 along with James Joyce and the usual pulp fiction suspects.

Room 101? It comes from George Orwell's novel, *1984*. It was a much feared room where everything that entered it disappeared.

Q: SO THE CHURCHES WERE NOT BIG IN THE FUN DEPARTMENT?

A: The RC church, not content with the Ten Commandments, created six of their own, including the compulsion to attend Mass every Sunday, receive Communion at least once a year (which, by extension meant having to go to Confession, thus placing the penitent firmly back in the clutches of the priest) — these and others had to be obeyed under pain of 'mortal sin' (a biggie that could consign the sinner to hell, unlike a 'venial' sin which only merited a longer stretch in that other Catholic creation, Purgatory). Then there was a whole raft of disciplines just to remind you who was boss. Attend Mass on holy days of obligation, refrain from meat on a Friday, fast during Lent, abstain from food before Communion, not forgetting fast days, rogation days, novenas, scapulars, miraculous medals, sodalities, retreats, benediction and that inspired sales gimmick, Limbo.

Q: LIMBO? A SALES GIMMICK?

A: Yes, the story went that if someone died before they were baptised they could not enter the gates of heaven but were consigned to Limbo. Who decided on this piece of cod theology God only knows but the plot was cunning. Parents rushed to get their children baptised as soon after they were born as possible, just in case of an early death when the pearly gates might just clang shut.

Yes, it is hard to believe that an all-loving, infinitely merciful God would be at the gates directing some recently deceased infants to some celestial waiting room. But the plot was to obtain the desired result of getting more baby Catholics through the baptismal turnstiles more quickly.

Q: WERE THEY SO EXTREME IN ENGLAND?

A: Much less so in England, where the culture of a laissez faire Church of England had the strongest influence. Also, in

England most Catholics went to Mass because they chose to, whereas in Ireland if they didn't they might get talked about. Neither was the sexual repression so pronounced and the censorship of books, magazines or movies was of a much more liberal nature. Scotland, too, never quite felt the same severity of Catholic dogmatism as across the water but it did have sway in cities like Glasgow.

How? To cite one example, in more liberal Edinburgh, prostitution works very well through the existence of some 20 or so sauna and massage premises. Some of them are very good too (... or so one hears ...) as girls are safe, warm and not exposed to the dangers of cold, dark streets and potentially disturbed and violent men.

The police are not too concerned and the local residents are happier than if the girls were walking the streets with all the concomitant problems of kerb-crawling, friction and abusive exchanges. However, in Glasgow with its strong Catholic influence, such premises are rare and susceptible to raids.

Q: BUT IF PROSTITUTION IS ILLEGAL, THIS IS BOUND TO HAPPEN?

A: Technically you have a point but in Glasgow, within a relatively short space of time, seven young women who were working the streets looking for punters have been murdered. Had these girls been working indoors with some form of security system in all probability they would be alive today. For most fair-minded people there is no moral dilemma. Which is the greater evil, licensing sauna and massage premises where prostitution may or may not take place, or forbidding such places and suffer the risk of young women being abused, robbed, beaten or even murdered?

Q: WILL SUCH CONTROVERSIAL FUNDAMENTALISM LAST?

A: No — the rate of change has been dramatic. Within a generation the fabric of Scottish society has been transformed. Up to the 1970s, Christmas Day was a working day and all the emphasis was placed on the secular New Year celebrations. Paradoxically, vastly more alcohol was consumed per head by Scots at New Year than their Christmas-celebrating southern neighbours would ever think of. However, the Low Churches seemed to choose to thole *Thole?* — Sorry ... suffer, endure, put up with ... these excesses rather than adopt the High Church (aka papist) feasting on Christ's birthday.

Church attendances were high but Sunday was a dreary experience with virtually no entertainment, shopping, sport or recreational facilities.

Q: DID THE LAW CHANGE?

A: Yes. Before 1976 Scottish pubs shut at 10pm and stayed firmly shut on the Sabbath apart from the hilarious bona fide exemptions. *Bona fide?* Yes, this rule allowed travellers who had journeyed a pre-determined number of miles the right to buy food and drink on the Sabbath. Hotels throughout the land would display a Bona Fide book where travellers could enter their name and starting point of their journey. *Sounds very civilised.* The concept was good but hordes of local males would swoop on the nearest inn or hotel and list their starting points as anywhere from Lands End to John O'Groats just to avail of the booze ban exemption. Wee hotels with half-a-dozen bedrooms would have bars that could cater for 100 thirsty punters. The law was an ass and everyone knew it.

All in all the Sabbath was grim and Monday to Saturday little better. Restaurants were few, café bars unknown and pubs all provided a spartan functionality with no fripperies such as darts or pub games or even food. Drinking was a serious business, tables were small, sufficient only to hold glasses and designed to discourage distractions such as cards or dominoes. Drunks were a common sight at closing time. The picture was pretty bleak. The wave of Asian restaurants had yet to come — in fact Babar's of Lothian Road in Edinburgh shared with Tonto the distinction of being The Lone Indian.

Q: THAT'S ALL GONE NOW?

A: Just about, apart from where the fundamentalists hold sway, and where the odd anachronistic exception can be found. *Such as?* The great swathes of 'dry' areas in Glasgow where premises selling alcohol were forbidden under feu or lease-owner restrictions on the use of the land. There's also one intensely irritating piece of legislation that was a senseless token to the churches when the licensing laws were civilised in 1976. Visitors might never be aware of this but you can go into any supermarket on a Sunday morning and buy all you need for a lavish Sunday lunch. Meats and fish of all varieties are available in abundance as are the widest range of vegetables, soups, condiments, sauces, puddings, breads, cheeses — the full Monty. But the shopper might be overheard:

What else do I need? Ah yes, a bottle or two of wine.
Sorry madam, you can't buy wine.
What?
We are not allowed sell alcohol till 12.30.
You're kidding.
No madam, I'm afraid that's the law.
Why?
Nobody seems to know madam, something to do with it being
Sunday.
So you can process my entire trolley of food through the check-out
but I can't select some wine.
No madam.
But if I come back at 12.31 that's okay?
Yes madam.

Yet another irony is that if madam were staying in a nearby hotel she could drink herself stupid waiting for the supermarket curfew to end, but a non-resident in the hotel bar would have to wait for the mysterious hour of 12.30 to arrive before being served a drink.

Q: WHERE'S THE LOGIC OF NO BOOZE SALES TILL 12:30?

A: There is no logic, it is more a token gesture to the churches. Presbyterianism in general and the fundamentalist wing in particular have always disapproved of alcohol. In fairness, its consumption can be highly destructive especially in Scotland. Alcohol can be directly related to road accidents, fights, stabbings, domestic violence, murder, fires, domestic accidents, job losses, divorces, in fact the whole panoply of human misery. Also, the Celtic genetic structure seems to carry an in-built weakness for the stuff. All the 'great' drinkers appear to be Celts — Richard Harris (Irish, dead), Richard Burton (Welsh, dead), Billy Connolly (Scots, now teetotal, alive), Peter O'Toole (Irish, alive, but for how long?), Andy Stewart (Scots, dead), Dylan Thomas (Welsh, dead), Brendan Behan (Irish, dead) — to name only a few of the better known.

Q: IS THERE A BIBLICAL CONDEMNATION OF ALCOHOL?

A: There seems to be little scriptural evidence for the condemnation of alcohol, and Christ's first miracle was turning water into wine (and the very best stuff at that) so we must deduce that the Kirk's disapproval is based on the damage drink can do to society. But you ask about logic. If alcohol is intrinsically evil then it is evil from Monday through Sunday. ***And why is it acceptable to*** *buy it in a pub all day or in a supermarket on a Sunday afternoon but not a Sunday morning?*

One view is that because the main church service is normally at 11am, finishing around noon, worshippers popping into the shops after church would not see drink being bought.

But surely the bottles would be visible on the shelves?

Of course.

And if the bottles were intrinsically offensive they're going to be seen anyway?

Quite.

What if the worshippers don't disapprove and want a bottle for themselves?

They can't have one either.

Q : WHY DON'T PEOPLE COMPLAIN ABOUT SUCH NONSENSE?

A : It is part of the British character really. It took England some 13 years after Scotland to do away with the mid-day compulsory break of three hours which was introduced by Lloyd George during WWI to ensure there was no slackening of the war effort. Incidentally, the knock-on effect of civilised licensing laws is that the standard of pubs has improved beyond all recognition with many of them serving first-class food. Restaurants have had to try harder and the quality and variety of eating places has increased a hundred fold.

Brits tend not to complain. Not only the Scots but the English too had all sorts of arcane and archaic Sunday observance laws. At one time shops could only sell perishable goods on a Sunday but not tins or packets of food. Newspapers and magazines were okay as they were 'perishable' because their date gave them a finite life. One MP pointed out that he could buy a pornographic magazine on a Sunday but not a bible as the latter was non-perishable while the former had a limited shelf-life.

Q : SO THE CHURCHES NOW HAVE VERY LITTLE INFLUENCE?

A : Very little indeed and lessening. The Roman Catholic cathedral of The Good Shepherd at Dalmilling in Ayrshire — part of the oldest RC diocese in Britain was almost closed in 2002 and would have been the first Roman Catholic cathedral to close since the Reformation. The combined attendance at the two Sunday Masses seldom exceeded 50 — in a building capable of seating 700. The cathedral needed repairs which ran to £100,000 — to quote Bishop Maurice Taylor — and with such a small congregation the repairs were simply not realistic. The only thing that reprieved the cathedral was the decision by the Vatican that Taylor should soldier on and leave the problem to his successor.

The average age of Catholic priests in Britain is now the highest it has ever been and the amount of young blood on the horizon is both negligible and wholly insufficient to replace the existing clergy. While Rome sternly refuses to accept women priests and insists on celibacy for the men, the church is slowly bleeding to death. Even if a new pope swept away all the old constraints (none of which are biblical) it would be too late because most of the parishioners are either too old or too disenchanted with the church to care. Even in once devout Ireland attendance at mass has dwindled year on year and amongst the young, church-going is now the exception.

In the Church of Scotland numbers have been declining since the 1960s while the Anglican Church in England has recorded a 22% drop in attendance figures in just one decade, the 1990s. One positive comment for the Church of Scotland came from spokesman Alan Ross, '50 years ago people went to church because they felt they ought to, now people go because they want to'. As they say in the military, 'one volunteer is worth ten detailed men'. Despite Mr Ross's optimism the future of Christianity looks pretty bleak. Even the 'happy clappy' Pentecostal wing is in decline having experienced a surge of enthusiasts who were looking for something more cheerful and animated. Many argue that the churches have only themselves to blame. Any fun-loving agnostic of the modern generation who wandered into the standard church service with its incomprehensible language and mournful hymns would not be expected to dally long.

Q: WHAT DOES THE FUTURE HOLD?

A: Probably further decline. In May 2003 the figure for church attenders dropped below 10% of the Scottish population for the first time. However, saner voices are emerging. The Scottish Churches Initiative for Union group is an ecumenical body who sees the only way forward as through Christian unity. SCIFU produced a report in January 2003 advocating a merging of the Church of Scotland, the Scottish Episcopal Church, the United Reformed Church and the Methodists as a single religious institution. Alas, the General Assembly of the Church of Scotland's ruling body in May 2003 rejected the SCIFU proposal by 384 to 99 votes.

Q: No Catholics in SCIFU?

A: Afraid not. Whether we (or they) like it or not, the RCs have always taken the line that they are the one true church and all the rest are, at best, their separated brethren. *At best?* Yes, not too long ago, the others were looked upon as heretics who couldn't enter the gates of heaven. So separated brethren is considerably more mellow, if a tad patronising.

Q: So what did this SCIFU come up with?

A: Their report which was seven years in the making was partly a Christian desire for unity and partly a hard pragmatic acknowledgement of the need for survival. *Seven years?* It does seem a long time to come with something that must seem patently obvious but, sadly, there are still many negative voices around. *Such as?* Take one, the Very Reverend James Whyte, a former Kirk Moderator, who described the proposed merger as 'divisive'. Yes, yes, we know — don't ask. *How could a move for unity be divisive!* You would have to ask the Very Reverend gentleman himself.

Q: If religion is on its last legs why is there this Protestant v Catholic thing?

A: Ah dear! Wouldn't you like to know about our national food and drink or our transport infrastructure or perhaps our arts? *Maybe later, what's all this orange and green hostility?* This calls for another large dram and an easy chair. Comfortable? As with much of our turbulent history this goes back to the Reformation. Once Protestantism became established in Britain as a whole, Catholics were generally treated as second-class citizens. For much of the 17th century Catholics were the object of popular fear and suspicion. This was not helped by acts such as Guy Fawkes' attempt to blow up Parliament in 1605. Catholics were denied various civil rights until Catholic Emancipation in 1829. Restrictions on ownership of property were lifted and universities were fully opened to them in 1871. Even then they were not to be admitted to offices such as regent, lord chancellor or lord lieutenant of Ireland and the proscription from marrying into the royal family remains to this day. Although this is sectarian there is some logic here. If the monarch is to be head of the Church of England then the prospect of a Catholic heir presents a problem as would the role of a Catholic regent deputising for a Protestant monarch.

Q: BUT THIS WOULD NOT CAUSE SUCH SECTARIAN VIOLENCE?

A: No, the Orange and Green antipathy is mainly a Scottish (more precisely West of Scotland) and Northern Irish affliction. Scottish Presbyterians had a strong distaste for the whole concept of High Church structure and ritual and many would not even view the Church of England as Protestant but see it more as the name Anglo-Catholic suggests. The retention of archbishops, bishops, mitres, crosiers, vestments, high altars and much of the elaborate ritual associated with Roman Catholicism was not to the liking of the followers of Knox and Calvin. In England, the followers of Calvin became known as Puritans. Just one trivial example of Puritan disapproval was that they forbade the consumption of plum pudding as it was 'too rich for God-fearing people.' Under what was a repressive Anglican regime, many Puritans chose exile in New England and the Netherlands.

Q: WAS THIS THE ROOT OF NORTHERN IRELAND'S PROBLEMS?

A: The initial Plantation of Ireland in the 1570s and 1580s never really took off. The first 'Planters' had mixed success when they settled in Ireland's eastern and southern provinces, Leinster and Munster. The western province, Connacht, was too barren. However, the northern province Ulster had some prime land which was divided into parishes and granted to 'undertakers' who introduced settlers, partly from England but mainly from Scotland. The latter were mainly Presbyterians in search of religious freedom. The seeds of the orange and green divide were sewn. The Presbyterians had a natural antipathy to all things Catholic — Roman or Anglo, purely from a spiritual or doctrinal standpoint. But add to this their occupancy of lands that had been taken away from the indigenous Irish Catholic population and you have a double divide, a usurper/dispossessed divide and a religious divide. The aboriginal Irish were sent 'to hell or to Connacht' (the barren province) to use the contemporary phrase, very much in the same manner that Highland Scots were to be cleared from the land in the 19th century.

Q: HENCE THE ORANGE AND GREEN DIVIDE?

A: Yes, the term Orange came from William of Orange. He defeated the Catholic Jacobites on Irish soil at the Battle of the Boyne in 1690. This battle became the centrepiece of sectarian folk history. Ironically, the pope was on the side of King Billy and had church bells rung at James' defeat. **Why?** James was in alliance with the French and the Vatican was very much against further French expansion in Europe.

Q: WHY HAS IT BEEN SO BITTER?

A: Wherever the have/have-not situation has arisen, whether with the native American, apartheid or the Israeli-Palestinian conflict, the bitterness is most acute. Certainly the Irish carried out brutal attacks on the incomers and many a Protestant man, woman and child were murdered but these actions cannot be seen in isolation and must be viewed in the context of the sense of grievance of the dispossessed. The usurper can be all the more cruel because of the very probity of the case of the have-nots. Although the Catholics became a minority in the new Province of Northern Ireland, the Protestants also saw themselves as a minority — a six-county minority surrounded not only by the Catholics in the nine counties of Ulster but by the other 23 counties. They developed a form of siege mentality which continued after Partition when six counties of Ulster became Northern Ireland and the remaining 26 counties became the Irish Free State.

In Scotland the religious division remained primarily a doctrinal one and there was none of the sectarian killings of Ulster nor the no-go areas of divided housing that has cursed Northern Ireland for so long. However, the division didn't remain purely doctrinal. Waves of Irish immigrants came into Scotland during the famine years and the flood continued when the Industrial Revolution needed more and more workers on the Clyde and in the mines. Such was the influx that the Church of Scotland spoke out against the Catholic hordes being a threat to their Protestant faith. There were calls for repatriation and rallies in Edinburgh to agitate against the incoming papists.

This situation was further exacerbated by the constant exchange of shipyard workers between Belfast's Harland and Woolf and the 65 shipyards on the Clyde. The sectarianism of not employing Catholics in Belfast began to spread to Scotland. The existence of separate Catholic schools in Scotland made it easier to identify the background of job applicants. The question, 'what school did you go to?' took on a quite sinister undertone. In the rest of Scotland and especially in Edinburgh, the question might be used to ascertain social class but in west central Scotland, academic history was often only of secondary interest. Marches by the Orange Order became common and behind all the superficially innocuous claims about 'the right to walk the Queen's highway' there was a deliberate intention to convey Protestant superiority to the growing number of papist immigrants. So the flame of sectarianism was kindled in Scotland, fanned by the furnace blast from across the Irish Sea.

Q: What about the indigenous Scottish Catholics?

A: Good question. Native Scots Catholics were never subjected to such forms of Protestant triumphalism or aggression because their numbers were so few. They were also concentrated in the more remote parts of Scotland. It was due to their very remoteness that the Reformation failed to reach them. Barra for instance is one of the least accessible of the Outer Hebrides; it was untouched by the new religion and remains almost entirely Catholic to this day, as does South Uist and a large stretch from west of Fort William to Mallaig. The islanders would speak the same native Gaelic tongue as their Presbyterian brethren and their lifestyles would be identical. The divide would therefore be almost cosmetic unlike the immigrant Irish who were often near destitution, had a different cultural background and, even with Irish Gaelic speakers, had a tongue which varied greatly from the Scots Gaelic.

Q: So these were as much turf wars as anything else?

A: Very much, most turf war participants need a handle for identification purposes. The fundamental divide is between the haves and the have-nots. When the first West Indians flocked to places such as Brixton or Notting Hill in London, there was never any trouble so long as there was full employment.

Even people of the same religion and ethnicity can feud, such as in post-Wall Germany, when the impoverished 'Easties' began to threaten the jobs of the more affluent 'Westies'. In Scotland and Northern Ireland the religious divide made identification easier. The Scottish worker lived on little more than subsistence level and the incoming Irish were often seen as a threat to jobs or as the cause of low pay rates. Add to this an often hostile Church of Scotland and the situation becomes volatile.

Q: Where do the football teams Celtic and Rangers come into all this?

A: In Scotland, what began as a reasonably high-minded division became tarnished by the festering hatred found in pockets of Northern Ireland. The focus for the divide fell on two football teams. As Barcelona became a focus of Catalan anti-Franco passion, so the beautiful game became embroiled in the sectarian divide in Scotland. Near the end of the 19th century a soccer team was formed in the East end of Glasgow by a member of the Marist Order, Brother Walfrid. His motives were good; keep kids off the street, occupy them, give them a purpose, raise some money for charity and the local community and help feed the poor. He suggested the name of Celtic for the club and this was adopted when it was formed in 1887.

Although the description Celtic embraces Scots, Irish, Welsh, Cornish and Bretons, its main association in Scottish minds is with the Irish because the good brother and most of his young charges were of Irish origin. Because of its Irish – and by extension, Catholic – affinity, non-Catholics chose to identify with another team, Glasgow Rangers, just next to the shipyards of Govan. Over time these two teams grew into the Scottish giants they remain today. They became the focus of the sectarian divide both in Scotland and in Northern Ireland.

Q: SURELY NOW IN THE 21ST CENTURY NOBODY TAKES THIS TOO SERIOUSLY?

A: Certainly things are not as bad as they were but people who have been to what is known as an 'Old Firm' match will attest to the raw hatred which exists between the more sectarian elements of the crowd. One anomaly is that, although the divide is ostensibly on religious lines, hardly any of the football fans attend any church. To put it into perspective, attend a rugby match at Murrayfield where Scotland might be playing the All Blacks, Australia, Ireland, Wales or even the 'Auld Enemy' England. Tens of thousands of people will stroll from Edinburgh's West End, stopping for drinks at the pubs and hotels en route to Murrayfield. The mix of supporters is total and the crowd will swell to 70,000. The Scots are attired in kilts and draped in saltires and lions rampant. The visitors are equally well decked out with their own national emblems. Faces are painted, songs are sung, hands are shaken, children walk with parents and the entire atmosphere is a carnival of good humour and anticipation of an exciting contest. There is none of the incessant foul language of the football terraces. The Welsh, Irish and French (and now the Italians) love coming to Edinburgh – and only marginally less so, the English.

While all football matches tend to be less good humoured, sporting and sophisticated, those between the Old Firm are so ugly as to attract only the dedicated — hence the spiral of ugliness. Grounds are segregated with more rigour than apartheid, coaches are even sent to especially designated parking areas, supporters are channelled through separate streets; all practices unheard of at the more grown-up rugby venues that have never been tarnished by ignorant bigotry.

Q: WHAT DO YOU MEAN BY SPIRAL OF UGLINESS?

A: It is a spiral rather like the school playground where kids search for the most wounding insult possible in their limited repertoire: 'Your mum's got a big nose', 'Your mum's is bigger,' 'Your sister's got a spotty face,' 'Well, your dad smells and your sister's got zits' ... you know the sort of thing.

For example, Celtic have historically flown the Irish tricolour in recognition of the origins of the club. So Rangers have adopted the Union flag (aka the Union Jack). One proof of the 'spiral' is that when Celtic played Porto in the 2003 UEFA Cup Final in Seville, many Rangers fans interviewed in Glasgow suddenly became Porto supporters. Both sides of the Old Firm reserve their most vitriolic behaviour for each other.

Q: WHAT'S THE UNION FLAG GOT TO DO WITH A GLASGOW FOOTBALL TEAM?

A: Nothing. That's the point — it is as opposite the Irish tricolour as can be found. The Celtic followers would sing the Irish national anthem or The Fields of Athenry so Rangers sang Rule Britannia or God Save the Queen. The real lowlife of Rangers scrawl FTP on walls.

FTP? Yes it means doing something unmentionable to the pope. The Celtic simians counter with FKB or FTQ — that alludes to the same intimate act with King Billy or the queen.

Latterly, elements of the Celtic supporters have begun to equate the historic status of the Catholic Irish in Ulster or perhaps in the West of Scotland with the Palestinians and now the occasional Palestinian flag can be seen waved at Old Firm matches. *So what did some of the Rangers' fans respond with? Don't tell me.*

You guessed it — the Israeli flag.

Q: ISN'T THIS ALL RATHER INFANTILE?

A: Totally, and it could just be dismissed for the vacuous lack of intelligence it represents were it not for the sheer numbers involved and the pointless violence it generates. In England there are some intense rivalries but nothing quite sinks to Old Firm depths. In the US such evils are unknown. Also, the spiral reaches levels of hysteria beyond FTP or FTQ. Some Celtic supporters adopted pro-IRA chants. The inevitable happened — some Rangers followers countered with support for the UVF. An added problem is that support for these two bastions of bigotry can be found throughout Scotland. This can produce the lunatic scenario of a

Rangers supporters' coach leaving some quite innocuous town in the East of Scotland where they ask the driver to play a tape such as 'Songs of the UVF'. The supporters, most of whom are awash with drink, will sing dirges about the hills of Co Down or Derry's walls when none of them have stepped beyond the borders of Fife or East Lothian.

Q: BUT IT MUST BE DIMINISHING?

A: Yes, the picture is not so grim now. Many parents won't allow their children to attend Old Firm matches lest they too become drawn into this nasty vortex. Where once Irish surnames were a clear indication of religious affinity, this is no longer the case due to generations of inter-marriage. First names have followed suit with names like Liam, Séan and Ryan all universally popular. Also with fewer and fewer people attending any church, the divide is more Pavlovian than religious. It is worth stressing that the regular church attendees all tend to be good Christians, devoid of any of the malice that afflicts the so-called religious divide of the football terraces. The death, alas, is a slow process.

Q: PAVLOVIAN?

A: You will recall that Pavlov's dog still salivated when the bell rang long after the link with feeding was broken. So now, with the churches empty, hostility consists of some tenuous historic associations or simply focuses on a vague hatred of the colours blue or green.

There was a time when all the Celtic players were Catholic and all the Rangers ones Protestant and virtually all were local men from Glasgow or the surrounding Lanarkshire area. When Celtic won the European Cup in 1967, the entire team was drawn from around Glasgow. Rangers kept the religious discrimination in team selection long after Celtic had abandoned it. The legendary Celtic manager Jock Stein (a Protestant) was once asked who he would sign for the club from two equally talented players, if one was Catholic and the other Protestant. Barely stopping to consider the question he responded, 'The Protestant. Because Rangers would never sign the Catholic.' It wasn't until the 1980s that the first Catholic player ran on to the field in a blue strip. One of the great ironies of mindless bigotry is that Rangers supporters may sing foul lyrics against Roman Catholicism yet their team now contains Catholics from Rome. Both Celtic and Rangers field many more players from abroad than they do home-grown ones.

Q: IS THIS HATRED VERY MUCH A WORKING-CLASS THING?

A: In the main yes. It is certainly more obvious in the deprived areas of the West of Scotland. Sadly though, there is a sizeable contingent of the middle class who should know better but somehow get drawn into this out-dated and illogical bigotry. Their professional facades would not reveal these deep-rooted prejudices but they exist nonetheless.

Q: YOU MENTIONED EARLIER SEPARATE SCHOOLS FOR CATHOLICS?

A: At the peak of Irish immigration, there was a strong antipathy to the immigrants and their religion that was seen by many – including the Church of Scotland – as a threat to the Presbyterian faith of Scotland. Harsh words were used such as deportation and repatriation. The religion of the bulk of the Scottish people might be threatened or adulterated. The RC church eventually won the right to separate schools sponsored by the state.

The problem however was not that they were Catholic but that they were separate. Inter-school rivalry exists everywhere as does inter-town rivalry. Whether you separate people by eye colour, hair colour, skin colour, class, language, whatever — there will always be rumours about the 'other lot'. Add to this quite natural 'us and them' scenario the higher-octane ingredient of religion and the potential for combustion becomes all the greater. Especially in a region that has strong links with their fellow Celts across the Irish Sea.

Q: AS A VISITOR I FIND THIS HARD TO UNDERSTAND.

A: Quite. But bigotry never makes sense. Some sectarianism existed in the north-west of England in places like Liverpool where there was a substantial influx of people from Ulster but even there the Orange marches never had the sinister and violent potential of the Scottish or Northern Irish ones.

As for the US, it was the brilliant Rogers and Hammerstein who gave us that superb show *South Pacific*. You'll remember the tea planter played by Rosanno Brazzi who fell in love with the all-American Mitzi Gaynor character. When Mitzi finds out that her tea planter has been married before to a 'coloured' Polynesian woman who bore him two children, Mitzi cannot handle it, she breaks off the relationship and sings that memorable song, 'I'm gonna wash that man right outa my hair'. The bewildered Brazzi turns to the young US Lieutenant (who has problems of his own having fallen for a native girl) and the young sailor sings that extraordinarily brave and way-ahead-of-its-time song (this was in the 1950s), 'You've got to be carefully taught – how to hate'. This was probably the greatest anthem about bigotry ever written and in an era where racial segregation existed in many parts of the southern states.

Q: DID RELIGION HAVE A BIG INFLUENCE ON THE SCOTTISH CHARACTER?

A: Yes. It is probably easier to illustrate this with an Irish/Scottish comparison rather than a Scottish/English one. The Irish and Scots are from the same gene pool. The very word Scot comes from the Roman word for Irish – Scoti. Like a Scotch broth or an Irish stew there are many ingredients: Celt, Pict, Gael, Norse, Norman, Dane, with a few drops of Huguenot and Spanish – more so in the West of Ireland and the Hebrides – courtesy of the Armada. These two Celtic, expressive peoples gave the world jigs, reels and whisky, but one chose to follow Calvin and the other stayed with Rome. Why did the Irish cling to Rome? Probably because the British had dispossessed them of virtually everything else, the people clung all the more tenaciously to the old faith.

The Celtic temperament, the expressiveness and the creative genius remained, only the manner of expression diverged. The Calvinists disapproved of all things High Church and by extension frivolity, gaiety, and overt expressions of joy. Logically the opposites were to be preferred — industriousness, seriousness, diligence and, in a phrase, the 'Protestant work ethic'. This produced in Scotland a hugely disproportionate number of inventors (see chapter 2), scientists, medics, generals, financiers, bankers, philosophers and hosts of engineers (even the one in Startrek). Ireland is celebrated more for its expressive talents, notably literature, poetry and music.

There really is no difference in temperament, it is all a matter of conditioning and perception. To many Scots, jobs in engineering or science are proper jobs. Scots can be more inhibited about expressing their emotions. One interesting statistic is that the Scots send the greatest number of the gaudiest and largest Valentine cards in the world.

Q: BUT WOULDN'T THAT PROVE THEIR DEMONSTRATIVENESS?

A: You'd think so but it actually proves the reverse. The Scottish male needs the satin crimson heart and the gushing sentimental inscription because he finds it almost impossible to say the words himself.

Ricky Tomlinson, a Liverpool actor and Trade Union activist, had once served a prison sentence. During an interview on a popular TV chat show he described how he helped some of the less educated inmates with their letters. He was struck by the Scots inmates who, although they longed to be reunited with their loved ones, were incapable of expressing the endearments that they felt.

One of Scotland's best know columnists, Jack McLean, wrote of a New Year gathering he attended where the father of the house reached out and shook the hand of his bewildered five-year-old son at midnight saying, 'Happy New Year, son'. Of course with drink the floodgates can open and Scotsmen can be seen clinging to their fellow men and women in the fondest embrace pledging undying friendship.

Q: HAS SUCH CONDITIONING INFLUENCED THE POPULARITY OF SPORTS?

A: Other than in football team allegiance, sport was never influenced by any form of religious divide. The criterion for success will always be whether someone has the physical wherewithal to succeed. There is a tenacity and toughness in the Scots character that has produced some good boxers.

Poverty was probably the greatest moulding factor for Scotland's best footballers. Small men from nutritionally deprived backgrounds grew up playing ball games in very limited spaces such as wynds, closes and back greens. Their speed, dexterity and nimbleness developed into skills that were almost balletic, loosely comparable with the poor kids of Brazil who played for hours in bare feet on waste ground or the beach.

One conditioning factor in sport attributable to John Calvin is the classic Scottish football manager. These are a breed of men with craggy forbidding faces. Stein, Wallace, Shankly, Busby, Ferguson, Graham and others all maintained and maintain outwardly granite faces. It is not that they are dour or have no humour, it is simply the conditioning of the hard Lanarkshire work ethic. Even when overjoyed at a brilliant result for their team, the big smile that is beaming away inside just cannot make it to the front door. A slight lessening of the frown and a few terse words for the BBC might be permitted but a cartwheel round the touch-line would be inconceivable. Compare this with the delight on the faces of Irishmen David O'Leary or Martin O'Neill. Same blood, same genes, different conditioning.

CHAPTER 5
FOOD, DRINK
AND TOURIST THOUGHTS

Q: WHICH WHISKY WOULD YOU RECOMMEND?

A: The one you like best. Any Scotch whisky (or Irish for that matter, but spelt with an 'e') worthy of the name will be a quality product matured for a minimum period of three years. But there are malts from every region of Scotland, many of them displaying regional styles and therefore it is true to say to anyone who has claimed, 'I hate whisky. I drank it once and was sick!' that somewhere out there, there is a malt whisky just for them. There is also a mind-blowing variety of blended whiskies. Flavours range from the mellow and slightly sweet Glenkinchie which, despite the prefix 'glen', comes from the Lowlands of East Lothian to the distinct and, some consider, more biting taste of Lagavulin from the island of Islay. The Islay malts are generally at the heavy end of the peat/smoke spectrum (exceptions are some Bruichladdich bottlings and Bvunnahabhain) and the Southern Highland/Perthshire and Lowland malts are amongst the more fragrant and aromatic. Speyside malts are the most classic in style ... big, full-flavoured and long on the finish. But there are always exceptions to the rule. Some Brora bottlings (Northern Highlands) can pass for an Islay.

Q: WHICH IS THE STRONGEST?

A: All whiskies now conform to the percentage of alcohol scale that replaced the old 'proof' scale. The standard strength of whisky is 40% alcohol by volume (abv), though there are some cask-strength whiskies which can be as high as 60% abv. Glenfarclas still produces an over 60% abv UK trade bottling (105° UK proof) which corresponds to 52.5° US proof. Talisker malt is still bottled for the UK home trade at 45.8% abv.

Q: IF THEY ARE ALL THE SAME STRENGTH WHY DO PRICES VARY SO MUCH?

A: Very much as with wine. Most wines are around 12-14% abv but prices vary greatly depending on age, the branding, how expensively it is marketed and how much the Chancellor is taking in tax revenue.

Q: SCOTS SEEM TO DISAPPROVE OF PUTTING MIXERS INTO WHISKY. WHY?

A: When you pay your money it is your whisky and you can put whatever you like in it. It is not a breach of etiquette or snobbery to disapprove of mixers though, it is pure logic. Why add to a twelve-year-old malt whisky a lemonade or fizzy mixer that was mass-produced only yesterday? It does seem at best at bit contrary. Also, you will see visitors asking for some top-of-the-gantry whisky that they have never tried and they then add a mixer. If the point is to taste the whisky for the first time, why disguise the taste and body of it with what is often a sugary fizzy drink? At the end of the day, if it sells more Scotch, why should the Scots complain? Chaçun a son goût!

Q: WHAT ABOUT ICE?

A: Once again it is your whisky but if you speak to distillers they will advise against it. The temperature of the ice tends to suppress the bouquet and flavour of the whisky. It also suppresses your taste buds and you will be less aware of the true nature of the whisky. Incidentally, the same applies to these extra-cold lagers. Almost any second-rate beer of questionable quality can be sold at very low temperature, because the drink has no bouquet and is almost completely tasteless.

Q: AND WATER?

A: A splash of room temperature water in a malt whisky (or a blend) will have the opposite effect of ice and will tend to 'open' out the bouquet and flavour. The great attraction of whisky is its wonderful versatility. A blended whisky in a long glass with a liberal measure of water is an excellent drink to accompany any meal.

Half-and-half water and whisky is ideal for a session with friends. Take it neat if you are feeling a bit chilled. In Ireland, a hot whiskey is very popular for winter nights or if you are not feeling too good. A decent measure of whiskey, a spoon of sugar and a sprinkling of cloves, stirring till the clove flavour has infused – delightful. When adding water or taking a hot whisky use a standard blended whisky. Save your best malt for drinking on a special occasion. One word of caution regarding a hot whisky: do not use water that is too hot. The result is that the alcohol will vaporise and will literally get right up your nose!

Q: HOW COME SOME WHISKIES TAKE OFF BIG IN SOME AREAS AND NOT IN OTHERS?

A: In a word — advertising. In England, Bells is the big seller while in Scotland it is The Famous Grouse. In London, Teachers is a highly popular whisky, yet in Scotland hardly anyone drinks it. In Spain, the big sellers are Cardhu malt, J&B and White Horse. The size of the market share is directly proportionate to the marketing effort and the corporate affiliations. In India, Johnny Walker Black Label and Ballantine are two of the most popular. In Germany, there was once a fashion for Irish Mist, partly because mist in German translates as shit or to be more precise, manure. No accounting for taste.

If your interest in whisky is keen, you should visit one of Scotland's distilleries. Virtually all of them provide guided tours with an informative talk on the history and variety of Scotch whisky followed by an opportunity to taste a selection of malts and blends.

Q: WHAT EXACTLY IS REAL ALE?

A: It is a term deliberately chosen by natural beer enthusiasts to distinguish it from modern beer dispensed by CO_2 canisters. Since Roman times beer was brewed in these islands by individual inns and private houses. A fermentable carbohydrate (malted barley) was mixed with water (and additional sugar for greater strength) then yeast was added. The fermentation produced alcohol and the by-product was CO_2 that gave the beer its sparkle. Every village had its inns and pubs with in-house breweries. Because of market forces and the economy of scale brewing became more and more centralised with small breweries supplying several inns. As road transport advanced breweries grew bigger and beer distribution wider. The tens of thousands of breweries grew fewer and fewer as the mass-producing brewers grew bigger and bigger. The problem with natural beer was that because it was 'real' or organic, it – like milk – could go 'off' after a few days, particularly in summer. No problem for the micro-brewer who could brew as frequently as custom demanded. He brewed more beer in summer and less — though stronger — in winter. The old terms can still be seen in Scotland; 60-shilling ale, 70-shilling, 80-shilling and up to 120-shilling-ale. The shillings reflecting the strength and the duty to be paid on the barrel.

So what happened?

The modern beer barons longed for standardisation in beer. They wanted to do away with the huge variety of flavours, hopping rates, strengths, colours, textures etc. They wanted a beer which wouldn't go 'off', that could be transported hundreds of miles, tasted the same everywhere, looked the same, smelled the same and even if it could not be consistently good, was at least consistently mediocre.

Q: What did they come up with?

A: Lager. Yes, an alien drink to the Brits. In the early 1960s the only people who drank lager were women. It was always sold in bottles and served in quite elegant fluted half-pint glasses. Men drinking lager were given funny looks and drinking lager with lime was tantamount to coming-out.

How did the brewers overcome this prejudice?
The power of advertising. Lager had to be sold to macho man. Firstly they gave the product big butch names likes Charger and Norseman. TV adverts showed enormous great Vikings darkening pub doorways and embedding their axes in the bar top. Men were pictured sweating (in Scotland!) while working up telegraph poles or stepping off a boat from an oil-rig. The more macho the image the better. **Did guys really fall for this?** Hook, line and sinker. Mind you it took time but the propaganda worked. Old hand-pull beer fonts were ridiculed as old-fashioned. The new fonts were ultra-modern and illuminated. The publicans, however traditionalist, could not fail to see the benefits of the new drink. The new beer was inert, pasteurised, still, inorganic and crystal clear. It could keep indefinitely without going 'off'. All the publican had to do was link up the font to a cylinder of CO_2 and the beer was instantly gassed, fizzy, sparkling and never cloudy.

Q: What was the downside?

A: For those brought up on traditional beer, the new beer tasted too fizzy, it was served cold which kills any distinctive taste and while cold beer may be a must in Melbourne or Malibu it did not have the same appeal on a January night in Aberdeen. The other minus was that manufactured CO_2 from cylinders – unlike the natural by-product of fermentation – has a slightly gassy smell hinting of bad-eggs.

Q: So how did Real Ale make a come back?

A: It was started by a group of Englishmen on holiday in Ireland. They were drinking Guinness (before Guinness abandoned its natural product status) and they noticed how smooth and how hop-scented the beer was. They began to reminisce about how all beer in the UK once tasted and smelled just as flavoursome. This group became a lobby for the values of traditional beer that grew into CAMRA (the Campaign for Real Ale).

Was it successful?

Amazingly so; it is often called the most successful consumer lobby group ever. It seemed to strike a chord firstly with people of a similar age group but then caught on with younger people who had been weaned on fizzy lager. In some areas, real ale had almost completely disappeared. In Glasgow in the mid-1970s there were only a handful of pubs in the entire city selling traditional beer and they were all centred round the more smart and trendy environs of the West End. Edinburgh, with a long brewing tradition, retained more real ale pubs but the number declined to less then 5% of the city's total number of pubs.

Q: WHAT'S THE PICTURE NOW?

A: Mainly due to CAMRA but also because of a revival of interest in all things organic and natural, real ale has made a huge comeback and is now available in most major pubs. However, the rural and smaller pubs will probably stick with lager simply because natural beer needs a pretty constant demand to keep it fresh. Without the demand the beer will oxidise and go off. So, though many rural publicans would like to provide the service, it is sometimes just not realistic. The upside is that, in some remote areas and islands such as Orkney, Islay, Arran and Skye, small breweries have started to feed the local demand.

Q: WHAT IS DRAUGHT ALE?

A: Draught means drawn or hand-drawn and should relate to hand-pulled natural beer as opposed to being dispensed by gas pressure (CO_2) but the name has been misused. You'll see tins of beer with 'genuine draught' written on them which is a contradiction in terms.

Q: WHAT IS THE DIFFERENCE BETWEEN ALE AND BEER? AND STOUT FOR THAT MATTER?

A: There is no difference nowadays between ale and beer. Originally one had the addition of hops while the other did not. Stout is an old form of dark beer also known as porter because of its popularity with the porters of London's Billingsgate and Smithfield markets. Guinness remains the world leader in the manufacture of this product. Guinness remained 'real ale' for the longest until the introduction of what's known as nitro-keg. **Nitro-keg?** Yes, Guinness's most famous quality was its smoothness. CO_2 only made it fizzy and harsh which was anathema to the product's creamy image. Nitro-keg was a mixture of nitrogen and oxygen which when added to an inert beer, instead of just adding fizz it reproduced very much the original creamy texture. Nitro-keg is now used in many other beers to achieve that creamy quality.

Q: IS GUINNESS AT ITS BEST IN IRELAND?

A: At one time a pint of Guinness pulled in Dublin was more likely to be at its best than in a British pub. Now with nitro-keg dispensing, standards everywhere are pretty uniform. The popular belief of Ireland's superior Guinness still remains but any superiority is not rooted so much in the product as in the sheer volume of sales in Ireland and in the respect and knowledge of both drinker and bar staff alike. Also, in Ireland there has long been a barman's trade union which ensured staff were better protected, better paid and better trained whereas in the UK anyone can walk behind most bars with minimal knowledge, hence the large numbers of Aussies, Kiwis and South Africans who come and go behind our urban bars

Q: WHERE'S THE BEST PLACE TO EAT?

A: Naturally it will depend on what you want, but the general rule is if you want a bed go to a hotel, if you want a meal go to a restaurant and if you want a drink go to a pub. This is not to say that there are no good bars or restaurants in hotels nor that there is no good pub grub. Neither does it imply that there are no good inns with decent accommodation. Rather, it states the obvious – that people do best at what they specialise in. Also proprietor-run establishments are normally better than chains. Italian and Asian restaurants are normally proprietor or family operated, consequently the welcome and standard of service is generally of a high order.

Q: WHAT IF THERE AREN'T ANY SUCH PLACES?

A: Scottish catering has improved beyond recognition since the watershed year of 1976 but there can be a problem in more remote areas. Often the only place to eat might be a local hotel. The situation can be made worse by the fact that catering for tourists is a seasonal business and staff may change from season to season. Sadly, the welcome can be less than overwhelming and the first visual impression the visitor may receive is staff looking at their watches as you sail into the dining room at 8.45 pm. The scapegoat is invariably 'the chef'.

'The chef finishes at nine,' is all too often the first words of greeting the visitor hears. Also, the range of food available diminishes with each succeeding minute. The other doom-laden greeting, especially for the hungry outdoor types, is, 'Sorry, the kitchen's closed.' What is particularly aggravating about this stonewall approach is the complete absence of sorrow in the voice of the speaker – there may even be a hint of triumph. Should you have the naiveté, temerity even, to respond, 'But it's only nine of o'clock,' don't expect a heart-rending explanation of the difficulties of rural catering, more likely the statement will be repeated with the volume increased — 'Sorry, the kitchen's closed'. Not even a pretence of sorrow this time and just a suggestion that the addition of 'Are you deaf?' might be missing.

Q: BUT NINE O'CLOCK?

A: Yes, yes, don't say it — the whole of Europe from Prague to Lisbon is still in the shower relishing the thought of a few drinks followed by a leisurely dinner. Even the Americans and Canadians who eat relatively early find this hard to grasp. However, it is very much a rural problem and the letters of complaint in our national press are written by visitor and native alike. We are coming to grips with the tourist industry but we still have a long way to go.

Q: WHY DO THE BRITS HAVE PROBLEMS WITH CATERING FOR TOURISM?

A: This is now very much a thing of the past though the reputation may persist. There are several factors but one abiding reason was the British inability to disassociate service from servility that found its roots in the once all-pervasive class divisions of these islands. Historically, everyone knew their place. Restaurants were for the middle and upper classes and the proles considered them not for the likes of us. Pubs – mainly in England – were divided into the lounge bar, saloon bar and public bar and each stratum of society entered the environment in which they felt most at home.

Railway carriages were allocated for classes of passengers i.e. first, second, third and even fourth. The homes of modest bourgeoisie had domestic servants. So the whole concept of service was indistinguishable from the servile role. Though we have left most of this behind, this was part of British conditioning.

Q: IS THAT WHY THERE WERE SO FEW BRITISH RESTAURANTS?

A: In a word, yes. As the class structure of post-war Britain began to collapse, the association of service and servility remained. Service was never any problem to the American or Aussie I'm-as-good-as-you-any-day mentality. Aussie taxi drivers could take exception to passengers who sat in the back of the cab. 'D'you think I've got leprosy mate' was a common response. The same drivers were reluctant to take tips as they felt the practice was demeaning. The American caterer who enthuses with a big smile, 'Hi, I'm Chris — I'm looking after your table this evening' or 'Enjoy your meal,' means it. The US dollar spender expects good service as a right (as we all should); the concept of servility is an alien one. Some Brits still have difficulty with it.

Even when they are taught scripts (often based on US usage) such as, 'Good morning, Hotel Imperial, Sharon speakin' — how may I help you please' — it still doesn't sound right. Also, why the 'how' and why the 'please'? 'May I help you?' is both polite and clear. The 'please' is grammatically askew and makes semantic nonsense. This latter scripted greeting has now been updated to the even more cumbersome, 'Good morning etc etc ....' concluding with 'how may I direct your call?' (Haven't heard it yet? You will.) Who writes this stuff? What human being in the history of telephonic communication has ever asked how a call might be directed? It is a ghastly word that might possibly have some currency in the Arkansas Hilton but it sounds so alien to UK ears as to be meaningless. Worse, the kids who have this gobbledegook drummed into them have so much to say that they rush this artificially elongated verbiage and the caller finds the entire greeting indecipherable. What is wrong with a friendly, clearly spoken, 'Good Morning, the Sea View Hotel'? The caller is quite capable of asking to have the call 'directed' to whomever he chooses or stating the purpose of the call.

The Malmaison Group of hotels has a sound philosophy; they reason that they choose staff for their personality and intelligence. To insist on a script inhibits their natural expression, therefore they leave it to the staff to greet people.

Some stores in the US went so far as alluding to shoppers as their 'guests' and the farewell took the form of, 'we're missing you already'. Fortunately this syrupy nonsense never made it across the Atlantic probably because the average Brit shop assistant would have collapsed in a fit of giggles.

Q: MOST OF YOUR TOP RESTAURANTS ARE STILL FRENCH OR ITALIAN.

A: There have been some British restaurant chains such as The Berni Inns and Aberdeen Angus Steak Houses but, though the dining concept was good, their demise was essentially staff related. The Italians and the French have no problem with service. They see it more as an art form, a spectacle, a piece of theatre. Witness a top Italian restaurant where the maitre d' inspects a knife then clicks his fingers for some minion to take it away. The fact that the minion may enter the kitchen, wipe the knife on the seat of his trousers then return with a shining implement is of no importance, the drama has been enacted. Or take the French flambé — a demonstration of the wildest theatricality. Even the gestures are reminiscent of a matador nearing the coup, but both restaurateur and diner enjoy the spectacle. Also, however skilled the waiter or chef might be they do not patronise their customers. If Wayne and Tracey are stumbling a little over the menu or wine list, the Italian will offer discreet advice and a reassuring compliment on a good choice.

In the early 1980s my publisher once witnessed an excruciating exchange in a nameless restaurant in Fort William. He was sitting at a table next to an elderly couple of moderate means out on their anniversary. The waiter asked if they would care for drinks and the husband simply asked for the 'house sparkling wine', which was a mistake as the waiter reappeared with Lambrusco and without ceremony popped the bottle and poured two glasses. The husband, clearly wanting to show his wife that he still had a wee bit of class asked the waiter if he could inspect the cork. The waiter who was both young and arrogant could not resist plunging a verbal dagger into the poor man's heart: 'It's plastic, sir' and promptly turned on his heels and left. Any continental waiter would have prevented this situation from arising in the first place.

Q: WHAT IF WE WANT A SCOTTISH MEAL?

A: Scotland has tried to capitalise on the quality of its produce. Few countries in the world have been so well endowed with salmon, trout, lobsters, scallops, prime beef, lamb, venison and game birds. Restaurants have opened using old Scots names such as The Howtowdie (a hen that has never laid) The Capercaille or The Coble (flat-bottomed fishing boat). Just opposite The Howtowdie in Edinburgh's Stafford St was Mackintosh's, specialising in Scottish dishes and furnished completely in the style of Charles Rennie Mackintosh. They all came and went while the old established Chinese, French and Italian restaurants just go on and on.

There is one form of British restaurant that manages to soldier on. They are usually run by upper-class types who have come down in the world. Their knowledge of food and wine is extensive and they manage not only to overcome the servility factor but actually appear to reverse it. They somehow are able to convey to their punters that it is they, the restaurateurs, who are actually doing the customers a favour. The punter is at pains to stress that their booking is in order when the Honourable Caroline demands to know, 'You have booked, haven't you'. Such places can normally be found in frightfully smart areas such as Buckinghamshire, Hampshire or the posher parts of the Home Counties.

In Scotland, East Lothian or Perthshire would be the venue. There is some flaw in the British character where people need to identify with or genuflect to their social betters. These rather precious restaurants will often dictate the terms such as providing only one set menu — take it or leave it. The presumption is that the food is so exclusively good, cooked with the finest herbs and wine and served with the most exquisite sauces that no punter would be so ignorant, nay audacious, to say 'I don't like it, just give me a plate of chips'. On top of this tyrannical 'you'll eat what you're given', is the 'you'll eat when I say you can' which, unbelievably, can mean a waiting list of months. Only the strongest of characters would go so far as to demand to see the owner to complain of poor quality but, in this form of Catch 22 situation, the strongest of characters would not be there in the first place. The very tyranny ensures a level of meekness.

Q: MOST OTHER COUNTRIES WOULDN'T PUT UP WITH THAT.

A: Quite. Why on earth would anyone endure such discipline. There are only so many ways you can cook a piece of meat. Also the maximum pleasure threshold for a bottle of wine can be reached at a very modest price, after that it is all in the mind (aka the price tag). Can the indignity of being dictated to be compensated by the finest haute cuisine? Even La Cupol in Paris will normally give you a table at short notice — if not centre stage but a table nonetheless.

No, it is a peculiarly British form of lunacy. **You mean like train-spotting and the fluffy dice?** Suppose so, albeit of a different genre.

Q: THE IRISH SEEM TO HANDLE TOURISM BETTER?

A: The Irish don't seem to have this service/servility problem. You may notice quite a high number of British hotels have Irish managers. The main reason, however, is that the Irish took tourism much more seriously than the Brits. In the 1950s and 60s Ireland was haemorrhaging its people through emigration. There was hardly an Irish family that didn't have a relative in the USA, Britain, Australia or any of the English-speaking nations. Ireland had a predominantly agrarian economy; it had no coal, no steel, no shipbuilding, no oil, no heavy industry, in fact none of the resources of the more advanced industrial nations. What it had was a huge wealth of goodwill from the rest of the world not only because of the Irish diaspora but also due to its sad and turbulent history.

Q: SO TOURISM TOOK CENTRE STAGE AS AN INDUSTRY?

A: Very much so. There is also the natural hospitality of the Irish and a national psyche that places great importance on humour, conversation and the *craic* or more simply, general enjoyment. Visitors to many countries will talk of the sunshine, the scenery and the geophysical features or the food, while visitors to Ireland tend to talk more of the people they met. This applies equally in Scotland where population density is very low and hospitality is all the more important.

Q: BUT DON'T THE IRISH SPEND MORE MONEY ON TOURISM?

A: Yes they do. It is not just down to natural charm or hospitality; *Bord Failte* or the Irish Tourist Board has had for many years a budget that is roughly ten times that of VisitScotland. The Scots regularly complain in the press and the media that whenever there is an international travel fair, the Irish stand is always bigger, more professional and more busy than many other larger and wealthier countries. Scots also complain that VisitScotland is merely an afterthought on the British Tourist Board's agenda.

Q: MIGHTN'T THIS STRENGTHEN THE CASE FOR INDEPENDENCE?

A: Let's not start that again. But it is a problem trying to decide what is a genuine Scottish grievance and what is just the chip-on-the-shoulder resentment of a poor relation. The Scots are quite competent at shooting themselves in the foot without any outside assistance or lack of it. *For example?* Well, using the Scottish tourism spend vis a vis the Irish budget there is too much focus on playing the poor mouth role and not enough on getting the basics right. *Such as?* The very things tourists comment on; littered streets, chewing gum spattered pavements, potholes in roads, traffic cones left on roads for days with no apparent work progressing, toilets, food availability, licensing laws and all the most fundamental elements which add to a holiday. In July (of all months) 2000, Aberdeenshire Council announced the closure of 69 public lavatories in a cost-saving exercise. Not one drop less urine would flow in that unenlightened place, it has to go somewhere. There are some economies which just cannot be made. The Scottish Tourist Board in 2001 spent valuable resources in recruiting a real hot-shot chief executive only to find he had conflicting commitments elsewhere making his appointment unviable. The 'out before he was in' CEO was replaced by another who promptly changed the most obvious, sensible and descriptive name of the STB to the characterless and vacuous VisitScotland.

Q: VISITSCOTLAND! NOT VERY IMAGINATIVE IS IT?

A: Worse than that, it is tinkering at the edges of what the industry needs when attention should be focused on the important issues. Also, changes in logos and titles involve countless changes in literature and presentation material, money which could be used more effectively elsewhere. Some slogans are staggeringly thoughtless. Take the one promoting the Scottish Borders. Some PR whizzkid came up with the statement that the Borders were 'Scotland's leading short break destination'. Local hoteliers and restaurateurs howled, 'imagine a quality restaurant being recommended for its sandwiches'. The term 'short break' went down like a lead balloon with catering professionals in the Borders. Just one example, the Southern Upland Way is a walk of great beauty stretching from Stranraer to Cockburnspath, a distance of 212 miles (340km). Walk that on a short break! Yet, despite complaints the unpopular road sign remains in situ.

Q: ISN'T THAT JUST THE PACKAGING?

A: Maybe in that instance, but we tend to be cursed with a 'can't do' attitude. In restaurants, bars and tourist facilities it is not uncommon to be told what is 'off', or that the premises close in 10 minutes, or that no-one can show you round the distillery/museum/castle because someone is 'not around'. We find it difficult to welcome people warmly and begin with some truly positive 'can do' options. The tendency to begin with an itemisation of what we cannot do still prevails.

Q: NO OFFENCE, BUT YOU BRITS ALWAYS SEEM TO BE SO FAR UP YOUR OWN ASSES!

A: There are still some hang-ups about class, accents, status and service. US Presidents all retain their home state accents but in the UK it has been the norm for people who came from, what were patronisingly called, the provinces, to talk the talk of Oxford and Cambridge. This produced a breed of transvoxites.

Transvoxites?

Same as transvestites only with voices. Margaret Thatcher, a grocer's daughter from Grantham in Lincolnshire would, as a child, have spoken like any normal kid, but after elocution lessons, she acquired an accent reminiscent of a theatrical duchess. Lords Jenkins and Parkinson, one from the Welsh valleys and the other, a railwayman's son from Manchester, sounded more like the hereditary peers they rubbed shoulders with. It is getting better all the time but, although ex-Prime Minister John Major spoke of a classless Britain, there is still some way to go. The Scottish egalitarian traditions have ensured that the adoption of airs and graces does not afflict too many folk and those it does afflict quickly become objects of derision.

Q: ACCENTS AREN'T A BIG DEAL IN SCOTLAND ARE THEY?

A: Not so much in Scotland. There's a saying that it is hard to sound pompous in a Scots accent.

Q: BUT THE SCOTS SEEM TO LACK CONFIDENCE?

A: A scientific analysis carried out by the World Health Organisation in 1997 revealed a great deal about the nature/nurture dichotomy. The survey was to gauge how confident teenagers felt about themselves. The survey was carried out in 26 countries — 25 western European countries plus Canada. Top of the list for confident kids was Spain with France, Germany, Sweden, Lithuania and Canada in the top ten. It would be interesting to see where the US would be placed in this league as US parents give their kids constant positive affirmations. Scotland alas, was in the bottom three along with Slovakia and Estonia. Spain topping the league was no great surprise. Spanish kids are hugged, kissed and cosseted by all from the parents through the extended family to complete strangers. Scots tend to put their kids down with a 'and what would you know' attitude.

Q: WHAT'S A TYPICAL SCOTTISH BREAKFAST?

A: Traditionally, a full British breakfast was to die for — (perhaps even literally in view of the fat content). Eggs, bacon, sausage, black or white pudding, tomatoes or beans, mushrooms, toast or fried bread with a large pot of tea. In Scotland there was usually the option of fish such as Arbroath Smokies or kippers. Until the 1970s this was normally included in the room rate. Slowly, through cost cutting, the continental influence and the cholesterol warnings, the full cooked breakfast became an optional extra. It is still usually available in B&B accommodation and if you are on a walking, cycling or activity holiday in Scotland there is nothing to match the cooked breakfast to set you up for the day.

Q: WHAT'S THE PROBLEM WITH KIDS IN PUBS?

A: Despite the liberalisation of Scotland's licensing laws, there is still a widespread reluctance to have children in pubs. The legislation is in place, all licensees have to do is apply for the appropriate permit (there are seven types) but not enough do so. Hotel bars are generally fine and many publicans have gone out of their way to make child-friendly environments. Some have established play areas where children are not just tolerated but invited to enjoy themselves. Alas, it is still not uncommon to see foreign visitors enter a pub with a child or two and be turned away. The look of bewilderment on the tourists' faces says it all.

It is a cultural hangover. It was not so very long ago that some pubs refused entrance to women. Drinking was a rather serious male preserve particularly in Scotland where pub games, food and too much comfort were frowned upon. The residual level of innate disapproval of drink is very much a Low Church heritage. The Welsh churches ensured that many councils denied Sunday trading licences to publicans so a family meal in a pub was not possible. The English were always more easy about children in pubs. On mainland Europe where alcohol is an intrinsic part of every day life such barriers are unknown and in Ireland publicans have been known to reprimand British visitors for leaving children outside the pub door or in a car. The good news is that it will all change shortly due to new legislation proposed for the Scottish Parliament in an effort to cut down on binge drinking and ensure that we present a more modern face to the visitor.

Q: LESS SO WITH THE ENGLISH?

A: Yes, English diffidence is more class-oriented. They will recount with embarrassment how an American visitor addressed a duke as, 'Hi, dook' though why any visitor should have deference to an archaic class system doesn't seem to occur to them. But there are so many facets; why should a 5ft tall princess be called 'Your Royal Highness'? Such peculiar behaviour has gone on for so long the Brits are inured to it. Years ago on entering the US Consulate in Edinburgh in the 1970s one was met by a large picture in the hall of a smiling Jimmy Carter in casual dress with an open neck shirt. At the base of the picture were just two words — Jimmy Carter.

The equivalent picture for some lowly British Ambassador would feature him in formal military tunic with cocked hat and plumage, shiny buttons, medals and as many accoutrements and insignias as possible. He would be unsmiling and the caption would read The Right Hon Sir Tufton Bumpton, KCMG, DSO, MBE, LLD, MA, VD, WC etc.

Q: IS THIS WEATHER TYPICAL?

A: Yes. Whatever the weather, it is typical. The four seasons in a day is not uncommon. Scots folk are used to it. Where it can be dangerous is for hillwalkers and Munro Baggers (q.v.) who are not used to the weather. One can leave sea level on a hot and windless day yet only 1500ft up (457m) the conditions can be life-threatening to the badly equipped. Once an American tourist returning home asked her Glasgow taxi driver who was taking her to the airport if the sun ever shone in Scotland. He replied, 'How would I know. I'm only 28.' The Scots have to be philosophical about the weather!

Q: NO HABLO INGLES. ES POSIBLE HABLAR ESPANOL? OR HOW CAN I GET ANYONE TO SPEAK TO ME IN MY NATIVE TONGUE?

A: Considering the numbers of tourists who visit the UK and the massive amount of revenue they generate, the British in general are sadly lacking in the ability to speak foreign languages. A survey carried out by the Scottish Centre of Tourism (SCOT) in March 2002 found that 97% of the people working in the hotel industry could not answer basic questions in French and German. Some hotel staff thought Deutsch meant Dutch.

What's the problem? To be fair, most countries teach English as a second language so just about all visitors have some English, whereas British schoolchildren can choose to learn French, German, Spanish or almost any other language. English in effect has become the international language; it is used worldwide in air traffic control, navigation and computer-speak. So, for the Brits, the incentive to speak a second language may not be as great as for other nationals. Another problem is that Latin languages are often very expressive. The native Brit is not very expressive in his own language so there is the culture gap on top of the linguistic one. Also, English is very easy to learn apart from some inconsistencies in spelling and pronunciation.

Q: WE NOTICE THERE ARE NO TRAINS TO THE AIRPORTS AT GLASGOW AND EDINBURGH.

A : Alas, another embarrassment. Although our trains rattle quite closely past Edinburgh and Glasgow airports, no-one planned a branch line into the airports themselves. In Edinburgh, we have black cabs that can take you to the airport but are not allowed to take passengers from the airport. **Who does?** White cabs, but – wait for it – when the white cabs return to the airport they are not allowed to take passengers to their flights. So the carrying capacity of the cabs is halved while the fuel expended is doubled. You will no doubt have noticed that fuel here is about five times the price it is in the US. Another frustration is that because of the government's short-sighted policy in the 1960s of shutting down unprofitable rail lines, many people in rural areas have no option but to drive to the airport to avail of the many cheap flights now on offer. The car park charges can now exceed the cost of the flights.

Thank you. You have been very direct about your country.

It is a national characteristic. Haste ye back.